It's Your Business…
A reference of ideas, tips and musings for entrepreneurs

R. Mickey Gorman
Brendon W. Sommers

ISBN: 1468042785
ISBN-13: 9781468042788

DEDICATION

To all of our "kids", who not only learned from us, but taught us as well.

CONTENTS

ACKNOWLEDGMENTS

We would like to acknowledge everyone that has had an impact on us. Obviously, there are a lot of them and many are mentioned throughout this book. Specifically, we'd like to recognize:

Ed Davis

John Gulick

Kathy Grey

Mike Hearn

PREFACE

We love dreamers. Those people that have an idea and that insatiable desire to be an entrepreneur. This book is a collection of some of the articles and white papers we've written over the years. We were asked to compile some of our best pieces and so we chose the ones that seemed to be the most popular by our readers, students and peers.

This isn't your typical self help book for entrepreneurs although most of the information and stories can be applied to your small business endeavors. This, as the title suggests is a collection of ideas, tips, strategies and musings from people that are entrepreneurs themselves.

We have spent countless hours reading, researching, coaching, teaching and counseling entrepreneurs and running businesses. Through all of this we have amassed a fairly large amount of information, statistics and our own real life experiences that we like to call "truths from the trenches". And we believe that the knowledge and experience we've accumulated over the last combined 70+ years should be shared with others, to help others.

You'll notice countless references to people and references that we've found have helped us. (They are not really countless, we just didn't go back and count them). But feel free to utilize the resources we mention. They can be as invaluable to you as they have been to us.

Each chapter is short, generally 3-4 pages. This provides the meat of the topic and lets you move from one topic to the next at your leisure and read 3 or 4 chapters at a sitting (particularly in the porcelain reading room) without taking a lot of time out of what is probably an already very busy day for you.

As we do with our Entrepreneurial Academy students, we always ask for feedback. If anything in this book has an impact on you, please let us know. Our contact information can be found at the back of the book. As a reader of this book, you become by extension, one of our "kids" and hearing from our "kids" is always welcomed and encouraged.

A ROADMAP

Anyone who has ever bought or considered the purchase of a franchise business knows they are not just buying a business name or product or service but a system of doing business. A business franchise usually comes with an entire set of rules and regulations on how the business is run. Most conduct extensive training in the culture of the franchise and how it works. Generally you get a business plan, a marketing plan, employee manuals, financial plans, market research….the whole kit and caboodle. In short you don't just get a business you get an entire business system.

In our entrepreneurial training programs we try to introduce students to an overview of a typical business system. We also introduce our classes to SCORE counselors to receive ongoing assistance with their budding businesses.

We know, however, from experience, that many small businesses don't take the time to develop a business system. They get it up and running and fly by the seat of their pants and thus, over half of small businesses fail.

And what about the businesses that succeed and it comes time for the owner to retire or move on to something else? Unless you have a documented saleable business system, you better plan on selling to friends or family. Any potential buyer who does what they call in the legal profession, due diligence, will be looking for a well thought out operational system. You can have great products and services and a brand with high visibility but have the "how to" all in your head. Unless you are selling yourself as a consultant as part of the business package, that makes for a tough sale.

Venture Capitalists, who invest in business start-ups, want to know beforehand what your plan is for an exit strategy. Any small business that has grown into a large business at some point has passed the reins of control on to someone else. It may be by succession in a family business or by bringing in new management, or by selling the company. The fact is the founder who had the big dream to start the business is not going to be there forever.

Anyone who has ever made the leap to start a successful business will tell you that at some point that business takes on a life of its own. The business begins to run you and the excitement that "birthed" your new "baby" wanes as it turns into a rebellious teenager. The competition becomes more intense, the economy takes a turn for the worse, your costs go up, customers' tastes change, your equipment needs updating, and your employees make you feel like you are running an adult day care center! As your business grows beyond your skills your enthusiasm becomes drudgery.

You can choose at this point to bail out by abandoning the business or selling it (if you can find a buyer). You can bring in consultants or new management. Or you can acquire the new skills and attitudes necessary to take your business to the next level.

Graduates of our Entrepreneurial Academies and other business owners asked us to consider developing a program to help take small businesses to the next level. We listen to our clients. We have started several programs including the Marketing Roundtable and Modern Marketing Seminars. We are currently researching doing online programs that folks can download and learn at their leisure.

ENTREPRENEUR OR JOBBIE?

Does starting your own business make you an entrepreneur? The answer to that is a simple no. Until you have built a business that can survive on its own without you, in other words, one that you can sell to somebody else, all you have done is create a job for yourself.

In her new book, The Entrepreneur Equation, Carol Roth describes most start up businesses as "Jobbies", a hobby that became a job. Much like Sarah in The E-Myth Revisited took her hobby of making pies and started a business that soon became just another job to her to the point of her hating to come to work each day in her own shop, many small business start ups are begun by folks who are good at something. The bookkeeper starts a bookkeeping business, the landscaper starts a landscaping business, the hair stylist opens a salon, the cook opens a restaurant, the plumber's apprentice goes off on his own and the cycle repeats itself.

One small business after another is opened by somebody with a technical skill and very little business skills. It is one of the major reasons over 50% of new businesses fail in the first two years of getting started. Folks take the skill that somebody else was paying them to do for them and think they have what it takes to make it on their own. It happens every day. And every day another small business shuts its doors because of a lack of basic business skills.

They have taken their time, talent, and treasure to maybe do something they love to do and simply made it into another job but this time with no guarantee of a regular pay check and probably no benefits. These folks are not entrepreneurs they are "jobbies". Entrepreneurs are folks who work not just IN their business but ON their business developing systems that can be repeated by others. They know that just like raising children their budding businesses need to be given roots and wings. If you have a lawn care business and all you do is cut grass day in and day out you are not building a business you are just working a job. And while you may enjoy the fresh air, the sunshine, and the smell of a freshly cut grass, if for some reason you were unable to do the job, you will not be paid.

On the other hand, if you had a fleet of trucks and a skilled crew who you had trained with your system of lawn maintenance, it wouldn't matter if you were sick and dying or laying out on the beach sipping a margarita. If you had a sales team out making calls on potential customers and great marketing materials as well as well maintained equipment and an office staff that can handle anything that comes along, you might well have a business and not just another job.

So many start ups are so focused on the job of trading their hours for dollars that they neglect the care and feeding of an independent business. Until they make the time to give their business a life of its own they don't have a business they just have a job that they own.

So take the time to ask yourself:

- Are you running a business or just doing a job?
- Where do you want your business to be in the next 2 years?
- If I wanted to sell my business, why would anybody buy it?
- What systems do I need to have in place to turn over my job to somebody else who does not necessarily have my level of skills?
- What training would need to be done to find someone who can replace me?
- What training do I need to take my business to the next level?

When you have reached a point where your business is running so smoothly that you can walk away from it, sell it, duplicate it, or even franchise it, then congratulations, you are an entrepreneur.

START UP

Did you know that in Charlotte County, Florida in 2010, with an unemployment rate over 13%, 1,549 new businesses were registered and that in Sarasota County, Florida 2,606 new businesses were born? Not bad, considering this amounts to more than 4,000 new businesses in a down economy, compounded by the onslaught of negative media coverage on the prolonged oil spill in the Gulf of Mexico.

Here's something else you may not know: More than 85 percent of those businesses were self-funded. Start-ups used whatever assets they had to get their businesses off the ground. They used savings, money from family and friends, credit cards, home equity, pawned pianos… you name it.

These entrepreneurs had an all-consuming dream of owning a business. Some may even have dishonestly pilfered a few things from existing jobs to set the dream in motion.

I'm not condoning theft by any means, no matter how big your dreams are, but we know it happens. Some folks using company materials — paperclips, pens and making unauthorized copies on the company copier. And some people spend work time working on a new business rather than working for his or her current employer. Think about it: When your dream business takes off and you start hiring people, don't you expect them to devote their time and attention to the tasks you are paying them to do?

Beyond that, entrepreneurs will do whatever it takes to make their dream a reality. And, I hate to tell you, in spite of all the "stimulus money" being tossed around in our nation's capitol, the chances of you, as a new business start-up, getting any of it is about as likely as your being signed as starting quarterback for the Green Bay Packers.

I was a SCORE counselor for years, and I love helping small businesses. But I cut back on individual counseling and recently resigned because I got a tad worn out talking to folks who came in looking for a handout. If you are looking for something for nothing, your chances of success as a business owner are dismal at best.

I've met with clients who say they want to start a business. When I ask them what type of business they want to start, they turn it around and ask me what type of business they should start and what grants are available to get it off the ground and if I'll write a business plan for them so they can get the grant.

I've often shared a formula for success: Focus times Faith times Effort equals Success. The folks mentioned above score a zero for Effort, and as we all know, anything times zero equals zero.

Remember all the talk about green jobs and green businesses and all the free greenbacks that were being tossed at them by politicians? Massachusetts gave

Evergreen Solar $58 million only to see them pack up and head to China for production. And, whatever you do, don't get me started on Solyndra! We had four students come through our Entrepreneurial Academy classes with green business ideas. Not one of them has successfully gotten their businesses started. The only graduate who actually has a green business came to class wanting to start a coffee shop.

What I'm getting at is that if you want to be a successful entrepreneur, you need to have a dream, and it needs to be something you love to do and have some talent for doing. Look, even the most well-run, well-documented franchise opportunity does not insure your business will succeed. We all have seen several well known franchises fail in this area.

So what do you need to do before you attempt to make your dream a reality?

First, take a look at yourself. What do you love to do that you can do well?

What is your passion?

Next, take the time to investigate and understand your market. Who needs what you have to offer? Can they afford it? What is your competition? What makes you different?

Then you need to find out what it is you don't know. What skills do you lack to succeed in business? Where can you acquire those skills? Who can help?

Finally, you need to get a handle on what the cost is of getting started and keeping the business running until it starts to show a profit.

Nothing will go exactly as planned. But I can assure you that failing to plan is planning to fail. You need to do the legwork and the homework. You need to understand the ins and outs and the pitfalls. If you are not willing to put in the effort, you will not succeed. In short, the locus of control in your business's success is you.

BABY BOOMERS BECOMING ENTREPRENEURS

A recent article in the Wall Street Journal, with information supplied by the Kauffman Foundation, points out that more and more new businesses are being started by baby boomers. The over 55 crowd is leaving the golf course and rocking chair (some would say they were "off their rockers") and becoming entrepreneurs. What's going on?

We have had several of these folks attend our Entrepreneurial Academy classes. The reasons are many. Some just need to work and can't find a job in their lifelong skill set. Some just want to do something with their time and now they have the time to do it having left the job market. Others just have an idea and they want to know what it takes to make it a reality.

We just learned that average life expectancy jumped up to 78. That means if you retire at 60 you can pretty much expect to spend 18 years.....doing what? As one of these folks, I can share my reasons for starting another business; and over the years I've started several, some worked and some didn't.

After 30+ years of running trade and professional associations in Washington, DC, I chucked it all and moved to Florida. I've been involved in sales for several

years as there are always opportunities for good sales people and honestly we are always selling ourselves
anyway. I volunteered my time in several Chambers of Commerce and joined SCORE as a mentor to small businesses also on a volunteer basis. Through SCORE, Ed Davis and I got together and started the Lunch and Learn and Entrepreneurial Academy programs in North Port. We spent two years developing those programs literally working for donuts! In 2010 we started Small Business Development Services, LLC. We were not just teaching budding entrepreneurs, we were doing it.

Having worked for years for nothing, or next to nothing, we had to bootstrap our business just like 85% of all start up businesses. We invested most of what we earned back into building the business (and donuts). True story…when the North Port City Commissioners voted to accept our proposal Ed and I looked at each other and said, "There will be donuts"!

So why did we do it? First we identified a real need. In a down economy with high unemployment, folks were looking for alternatives. As SCORE counselors we talked to dozens of folks who just wanted to start a business that they had the technical skills to do, but were lacking in the knowledge of how to run a business.

But to be honest, even though we have focused all of our time, talent, and treasure, into the success of the business, and we can sure use the money, we did it because it is what we love to do. We love to see our "Kids" succeed (we call all of our students our kids even the old farts like us). We love seeing dreamers achieve their dreams. We realize the future of our economic growth is going to come from entrepreneurs and we love the opportunity to help turn things around. If there is one thing I wish we could infuse in each of our students it is the passion we have for what we are doing.

Yes, we have had many obstacles thrown in our path and one by one we overcame them and moved on. And you know what? We have had fun in the process. When you are doing what you love to do it is not work. So even if you are over the hill, you ain't under it yet! Some of the top Fortune 500 companies were started in down economies. Colonel Sanders started Kentucky Fried Chicken in his 60's.

Got a dream? If not now, when? If not you, who? Nobody is telling you it is easy, and it won't happen overnight. So put down the TV remote, get up off the Lazy-Boy, and join us. We don't want to have all the fun by ourselves!

FOCUS

The Formula for Success....Focus X Faith X Effort = Success has appeared in several articles. I've been amazed at the feedback that I've gotten from friends. Several of them asked me, "Were you talking about me in that article?" I told everyone who asked, "Yes!" OK, not really, but to a certain extent it was applicable to each person who asked. Each of them had the same problem, Focus.

Even if you have complete faith in yourself and your abilities and the willingness to work your tail off, if you are not focused you run into the problem of mathematics where anything multiplied by zero always equals zero.
Faith and effort times zero = zero. If you can't focus, you can't succeed. Ten bazillion times zero still equals zero. You have a better chance with that lottery ticket and it will cost a whole lot less than investing in a failed business venture.

We make a point of telling anybody applying for a seat in our Entrepreneurial Academy classes that there is a big difference between working 40 hours a week for somebody else and owning your own business. You own your business 24/7/365 and if something goes wrong you can't say "It's not my problem" because it is yours and it doesn't matter what time of day it happens.

The biggest problem however with most budding entrepreneurs, according to them, is focusing on what they want to do. They have all these great ideas they want to put into action and if they choose one, they are stuck with it. They can't decide because choosing one excludes all their other options. So they dabble a little here and dabble a little there and end up with a big goose egg (that's a zero) in the focus part of the equation.

Let me suggest that the problem isn't so much what they want to do but why they want to do it. Business is commerce and commerce is the exchange of goods, services, and ideas. If nobody wants what you have to offer, you have nothing to exchange. If you don't believe enough in your offering that you can't make a commitment to it, then why would anybody else believe in it?

I can't tell you the number of folks who say they want to get into business to "make a lot of money". That's nice. Nothing wrong with making a lot of money. Personally, I've been rich and poor and I too have a strong preference for the former.

The next question is, "how do you plan to do that?" That question is followed by, "Why do you want to do that?" Frankly, to just make money doesn't cut it. I really don't care that you want to make money, I care about what I want. If you are not providing value to me, you are not getting my money.

There is a great lecture by Simon Sinek on Ted.com that talks about the importance of understanding why companies succeed and people follow great leaders.(http://www.ted.com/talks/simon_sinek_how_great_leaders_inspire_action.html)

In the lecture he talks about how successful people in business and life have a vision or a dream and not just a plan. He notes that 250,000 people in the 1960's, before email and Twitter, came to Washington, DC to hear Martin Luther King, Jr. say "I have a dream" not I have a plan.

Now, don't get me wrong, planning is an important part of making your dream come to fruition. But, planning is part of the how and not the why. The why is what gets you up and going toward the fulfillment of your dream. When you know why you want to do what it is you want to do, focus becomes crystal clear.

BAGGAGE

"Forgetting those things which are behind, and reaching forth unto those things which are before, I press toward the mark." Philippians 3 13-14

Things change. Always have, always will. If you don't adapt to change, embrace it, and understand it, like it or not, it will change you.

I joined SCORE right after the economic downturn and was asked to work with several small business owners who were headed for failure. They did fine in good economic times, but the world changed around them and they were falling behind. They just knew that if they kept doing what they had always done that things would work out. Things did not work out for them and they had to close their doors. Rearranging the deck chairs on the Titanic won't keep it from hitting an iceberg.

It pained me to see that happening. Yet, as the saying goes, you can't teach an old dog new tricks, and some of these folks were set in their ways. They were saddled with the baggage they brought with them. Right up to the very bitter end of their businesses.

Those folks who were able to accept that they needed to change things are easy to spot…they are still in business. Some are doing quite well in fact.

There is something in our make-up that strives to keep things as they are and are resistant to change no matter what the consequences may be. How many newspapers had to stop their presses and close their doors for good? While hundreds of papers were shutting their doors, Florida Weekly has been opening new ones and expanding its circulation. We just expanded distribution into North Port and Englewood and in the past year opened a new office on the east coast of Florida and started another west coast publication.

There is opportunity and with each new Entrepreneurial Academy class we start we see folks who are ready to make their dreams come alive. They are dropping their old baggage and pressing on to the new mark.

I was chatting with one of our students the other day and he told me he didn't have the confidence he could make it as an entrepreneur when he started the class. He is now starting to become a believer that he can do it. He, like all of us, was told growing up that you need to get your education and go get a job. More baggage to overcome.

Very few of us get told that you can make your job, not just go get one. We met recently with a couple of different organizations that are working to bring entrepreneurial training into the school system and we took a booth at the recent job fair locally to talk to students about owning their own business. During Global Entrepreneur Week we taught 5 high school classes at 2 schools and got great reactions from the students. So there is hope.

Another student in our EA class said she was reluctant to tell people about her business (in other words to give her 30 second elevator speech). She asked, "who would want to know about my business?" My answer was "Only the smart people, you don't want to do business with the dumb ones any way." I was telling her to overcome the baggage of fear of rejection.

Serious entrepreneurs don't just accept change they cause it. They get up out of the rut of everyday living and make things happen. They are proactive rather than reactive. They go (in Star Trek lingo) boldly where no one has gone before. They lead rather than follow. They know that if you are not the lead dog in the dogsled team, the view is always the same.

If you believe in yourself and in your business you want to tell everyone you meet about it. Fear of failure and fear of people (more baggage) goes right out the window. If you run into rejection you forget it and move on to the next prospect.

What baggage are you carrying that you need to get rid of to embrace change?

Things alter for the worse spontaneously, if they be not altered for the better designedly. ~Francis Bacon

E SUCCESS

I read a great book for entrepreneurs that we recently added to the text books we give to students in our Entrepreneurial Academy classes. (We get better, practicing continuous improvement with each class we conduct). The book is <u>E Myth Revisited</u> by Michael Gerber (the E stands for Entrepreneur). It is a great primer for anybody starting a new business and a tool for existing businesses to take their business to the next level of becoming a world class company. It teaches you how to work ON your business as opposed to working IN your business.

In addition, the book has a website (www.emythmastery.com) where you can login and download a multitude of worksheets for business planning as well as access a blog by the E Myth team of business consultants.

The subtitle of the book is "The Seven Essential Disciplines for Building a World Class Company". Gerber defines these as:

• Leadership

• Marketing

• Money

• Management

• Fulfillment

• Lead Conversion

• Lead Generation.

Gerber went a step further in his next book E Myth Mastery. The first part of the book deals with the interaction between Gerber and a client who owns a pie company. Part two gets into the specifics of the seven disciplines with links to the website for the worksheets available on each topic.

It is an excellent tool for business and it got me thinking about the personal side of entrepreneurship in addition to the technical skills necessary to run a company. Those personality traits that successful entrepreneurs have in common are Passion, Purpose, Perspective, Persistence, and Personality.

Passion and Purpose define your why. You have to have a strong belief in what you are doing and why you are doing it. It's called loving what you do. Perspective is your how; how you provide products and services and how they relate to the needs of your target markets. Persistence is your ability to persevere even when you can't see light at the end of the tunnel and things may not be going exactly as planned (and I can assure you, they won't). Personality is the positive outlook necessary to relate to others who you can help and can help you to achieve your dreams. It's the icing on the cake. Nobody wants to do business with a sourpuss.

Yes, money is tight and lots of folks are out of work, but the reality is the 85 percent of small business start-ups are self-funded, or funded with the help of family and friends. What better time to scratch the itch to start your own business than when you are unemployed or under-employed? It is as good a time as any to plan your work and work your plan.

SUCCESS TAKES EFFORT

I speak to a lot of audiences. I try to limit the presentations to those things I do best – sales, entrepreneurship and problem solving. As a rule I don't do motivational speaking unless the message is important and it relates to my areas of expertise. I think this message is important. Here is the gist of that presentation: Success Takes EFFORT.

E – Energy. It takes energy, enthusiasm and passion. It doesn't matter what you want to be successful at. You may want to run the World Bank (better you than me) or you may want to be a successful parent or a successful entrepreneur. You cannot be lukewarm about it. Have Energy.

F- Faith. You gotta have faith. You have to feel it in your bones. If you don't believe 100 percent in what you are doing, who will? Have you ever heard a CEO or professional athlete say, "I'm pretty sure I can do this"? Believe in yourself. Believe in what you are doing. If you can't, look for something else.

F – Focus. For years, I've heard my co-author lecture on the value of focus. As an entrepreneur, there are hundreds of opportunities to distract you from your quest. Business deals, offers, contracts, networking, audits, customers, etc, etc. If you let yourself become too distracted, the natural tendency is to wander. It's just like driving down the highway, taking in the sights instead of paying attention to the road and all of a sudden, you have no idea where you are. Now you have to take the time and energy to find your way back.

O – Objectivity. Granted, being an entrepreneur (or parent or artist or anything else you want to succeed at) takes a great deal of emotion. Remember the energy required? But you also need a certain amount of objectivity. You have to be able to step away from the emotional, if only for short intervals, to get a realistic perspective on your success to date. When you sit down with your accountant or attorney, do they get emotional? They understand the need to be objective. To bring a rational point of view to table.

R – Risk. Everything has risk involved. Insurance companies count on it. Entrepreneurship has risks involved. Generally, money is a risk. Yours or someone else's. Reputations are at risk. Health can be at risk. As an entrepreneur, you may have the instinct to go at it 18-20 hours a day. Trust me, this will take its toll on your health. Emotional risk. There are a lot of ups and downs on the road to success. Are your shock absorbers working?

T- Finally it takes tenacity. What's the point of expending all that energy, keeping the faith and taking risks, if you're not going to stick it out? Be a pitbull. Once you get your teeth into it, don't let go.

These are traits the we have observed of successful people like Lee Iacocca, Michael Jordan, Bill Gates and countless others. Put some EFFORT into your endeavor to be successful.

DREAM GIVER

I recently watched a great video that I picked up at the library, <u>The Dream Giver</u> by Bruce Wilkenson, who also has a book out by the same name. The video walks the viewer through the stages of getting from your comfort zone to

realizing your dreams.

He describes the comfort zone as being like a walled fortress we all hesitate to climb out of — even in the quest for a big dream. But as we look over the wall and see the big goal up on the mountaintop off in the horizon, we force ourselves to climb the wall.

Once over the wall and out of our comfort level, we run into "border guards." These are the family, friends and others who tell us to go back, there is no way you can make it to your dream. They tell you all your faults and attempt to get you to return to your comfort zone. Should you manage to get past the border guards, you enter the vast wasteland. The wasteland is the struggle that all dreamers must pass through in order to achieve their dreams.

Anyone who has ever started a small business will tell you about the frustrations of the wasteland — you try things that don't work and you must adjust accordingly. It can be a long and painful struggle, but the wasteland is what prepares you for what is ahead on your journey: the top of the mountain.

At the end of the wasteland is a resting place called sanctuary. It is a beautiful pool and waterfall where you can take a breather. (I'm guessing if there is theme music here it has to be Barry Manilow singing "I Made It Through The Rain.") Here you relax a bit and look up to the forest above the waterfall and see a bright light coming through the trees. You go to the light and see a great view of your dream across the valley on top of the mountain. Renewed and filled with new strength and vision to press on to your goal (and you are going to need it), you move into the valley of the giants.

The giants that protect the mountain are many. They come in the forms of government regulators, competitors, tax collectors and others who stand in the way of reaching your dream. One by one, you have to go over under around or through these giants. David and Goliath come to mind here, and you as the dream seeker will have to load up your slingshot and fire away.

Should you succeed in slaying the giants, you are now free to climb the mountain and embrace your dream. At the mountain's peak, you are able to look back at all the obstacles you had to overcome to get here. You can stop now and build a little town called New Comfort Zone or you can look ahead and see the next mountain.

In the Bible's book of Samuel, most folks miss the fact that the shepherd, David, asked three times, "What is the reward for the man who kills Goliath?" He was told each time about the great rewards. "The king will enrich him with great riches, and will give him his daughter, and make his father's house free in Israel" (Samuel 17-25). We all know that David succeeded in his goal to kill the giant and should have lived happily ever after. But no, that didn't happen. King Saul became jealous of David and tried to have him killed on many occasions. David had a few more giants to kill before he became king.

Nobody said that reaching your dream would be easy. What The Dream Giver says is that you can attain the dream after you do the work — and it won't necessarily happen in your time frame, but only when you are ready to receive it.

What you have to do is escape your comfort zone, sneak past the border guards, survive the wilderness and knock out a few giants. Simple!

LION TAMER

A true story! I was given a request for SCORE counseling by an individual who asked for help to start a business. When I met with him I asked him what type of business he wanted to start and he responded, "you tell me what's a good business to start these days." I suggested Lion Taming as he was going to be eaten alive anyway in any business he gets involved with. (OK, I really didn't say that.)

The reality is that for you to start your own business and make it succeed (particularly in a down economy) you really have to love what you do or be extremely lucky. I'm not discounting luck, unless you are rolling in dough, any start up can use all the luck it can get. But nothing will replace hard work and persistence. And when things get tough, and I guarantee they will, if you don't love what you are doing you will find it hard to persevere.

I love what I do. I love writing, teaching, and coaching small business owners. I love it so much I often do it for no remuneration (yup, for free). I've taught Junior Achievement classes at elementary schools and classes on marketing at the Imagine School and had fun doing it. I volunteer my time coaching several non-profit organizations and serve on a number of Chamber committees. I do it because I love doing it. I've been doing it for years and it is just now starting to pay off in a financial way. I've had tremendous support from friends and family to develop my business and could not have done it without them.

I'm not telling you this because I'm bragging or looking for another plaque for my "ego wall". My ego wall is in a plastic container in the garage. I'm just pointing out that when you love what you do that one meal of the day of microwave popcorn becomes a whole lot more tolerable.

I was talking with a friend the other day about the trials and tribulations a mutual friend of ours was having in her start up business. I told her what she was experiencing was only normal. Nothing ever goes exactly as planned and a winner (and she is) rolls with the punches and adjusts accordingly. She will be just fine. Sure she will be frustrated at times but she has the spirit it takes to achieve success.

That spirit comes from the success formula that I wrote about on several occasions of Focus X Faith X Effort = Success. The will to keep going in the face of adversity comes from loving what you do. Loving what you do gives you the faith to keep going.

The guy, who I really didn't recommend becoming a lion tamer, did not come to me asking for help to fulfill a dream, he was looking for an easy way out. For the record, I'd suggest inventing an app for a Smartphone game like Angry Birds if he is still looking. He just did not have the "fire in the belly" it takes to have a dream and make it happen. He would have better luck and lose a lot less money if he bought a lottery ticket.

I would much rather invest my time, talent, and treasure doing something I love than just working for money. Sure you need to earn money to keep going but there are too many people doing things these days that they hate doing just to make a buck. It shows in things like poor customer service or product recalls or even exploding oil rigs for that matter. I don't care if you are running your own business or working for somebody else, if you don't love what you are doing the quality of your effort suffers.

Over the years that we have been teaching our Entrepreneurial Academy classes we have developed a knack for knowing which students have a chance for success in their ventures. They have a light in their eyes and a willingness to do the work necessary to succeed. They can deliver their elevator speech enthusiastically because they believe in their dreams. They actively participate in class and ask questions. Their work is a labor of love not just laborious.

Thoreau said, "Most men lead lives of quiet desperation and go to the grave with the song still in them."
But he also said, *"If one advances confidently in the direction of one's dreams, and endeavors to live the life which one has imagined, one will meet with a success unexpected in common hours."*

DADDY'S LAP

When my daughters were little, my youngest daughter would often jump up on my lap and give me a hug when I was sitting in my overstuffed chair watching TV. She would get a hug in return and we would chat about things. Her situations solved or concerns taken care of, she would jump off and go about doing whatever little kids do.

Daddy's lap was a comfort spot for consultation and sharing of parental love. It also became an issue with my older daughter who in a fit of adolescent jealousy proclaimed, "You love her more than me!"

I pointed out to her that I loved both my kids with all my heart but that while she was more emotionally attached verbally, her sister was more in need of "touch" to connect to her emotional side. Daddy's lap was open to both daughters, as well as an occasional visit by Twink, our springer spaniel.

I share that story because I know what it takes to make a start-up business work and your time and attention can be so distracted by your efforts to succeed that you neglect to give lap time for your loved ones. I've told our Entrepreneurial Academy students that starting a business is like giving birth to a new baby. Just like a new baby, when the business is crying, you need to feed it and give it your time and attention. And like a baby, if you don't give your business what it needs in terms of your time, talent and treasure, it will not survive.

That is why it is so important that before you commit to starting a business you understand your "why." Are you starting this business to just make a lot of money? Are you starting it because you want to be your own boss? How about because you can't find a job with your particular skill set?

These are all reasons we have heard from our students. The world doesn't care what you want, and frankly neither does your business. Government regulators, competitors, customers, and yes, even family and friends, will pile on to your dreams and make demands on your time and you need to be prepared to devote the time to each required to get the job done.

Last time I looked in the city of North Port there were more than 1,680 businesses registered with the city and only 262 storefronts. That means the large majority — not including the hundreds of multi-level marketing and other businesses operating under the radar — are home-based businesses. It is a whole lot less stressful to operate a business where you have regular office hours and can go home. When your office is in your home, you can easily get in the habit of working at all hours of the day. Devoting all your focus to your business, you new child, can lead your family to conclude that you love it more than them. That's when it's time for some lap time.

Before you birth this new business baby, make sure everyone is on board with your dream. Sit down and discuss with your family and friends your "why." If your business baby is hungry or sick and needs your full time and attention, let everyone know what you are doing and why you are doing it and when you will have time to meet their needs as well. Then make time and do it. Maybe it's you who needs some time out on daddy's lap. Take time and get it. Don't work yourself to death, if you need help, get a babysitter. It may be a shock to your ego, but everyone is replaceable. Find somebody you trust and hand them the kid, diapers and formula, and take some time off. You don't have to do it all. Delegate!

.

IF I HAD A HAMMER

I like to tell the story of the guy who pulls into the mechanic's garage with a horrible knock in his car's engine. The mechanic opens the hood, listens for a minute, picks up his hammer, bangs on the engine block, and the knock stops.

The car owner is amazed but shocked by the bill the mechanic hands him for $100! He sarcastically asks the mechanic if he wouldn't mind breaking down the bill into details as all he did was bang on the engine with a hammer.

"Sure", the mechanic says and writes on the bill

Banging on engine with hammer...............$ 5.00

Knowing where to bang.......................$95.00.

We all bring to the table our own personal experiences and knowledge and deal with situations with the tools we have on our tool belt. Mazlow's Hammer states

"If you only have a hammer, you tend to see every problem as a nail."

Abraham Maslow

Dealing with entrepreneurs, I've talked to many folks who may be great doctors, plumbers, musicians, landscapers, you name it, they know their skill, they own their hammer. What they don't know is how to run a business. Marketing, bookkeeping, human resources, negotiating, sales, financial management, distribution and host of other business skills are traditionally not taught in medical school.

In fact, Dr. Chris Constance, Charlotte County Commissioner, told the graduates at the Punta Gorda Entrepreneurial Academy that he wished he had had business classes when he graduated from medical school. He noted that he set up his office, put in a phone system, hung up his shingle and waited for business to arrive. It didn't. He had to learn marketing, networking, advertising, and all the skills necessary to run a business.

There are two ways to learn anything, your own personal experience (The College of Hard Knocks) or through other people's experience (OPE). Learning through OPE can be a whole lot cheaper than mortgaging your house to start a business that may fail and drain away your life's savings. You can attend classes, read books, network, and go on line to gain new skills to add to your tool kit.

I have yet to meet a successful person who is not willing to share his or her experiences with an aspiring student. There are over 7,000 trade and professional associations were industry leaders do just that. When the student is ready a teacher really does appear.

FOF AND FOP

Two of the biggest things that hold people back from building a successful business are Fear of Failure (FoF) and Fear of People (FoP). Just about any successful entrepreneur will tell you that he or she has failed at one time or another and many will tell you they have failed more than once.

Starting a business in and of itself can be a scary venture. When you put everything on the line to start a business, failure is generally not an option. Attempting to do something or make something that is truly new and unique that people need brings with it a boatload of risk. Lots of things can go wrong. And I have to say, that's good. Fail early and often and quickly. Then move on.

When things are not working out as planned, you can do two things: adjust or accept that your plan failed and do something else.

One of the founders of Google, Sergey Brin, reportedly hums the theme from "Jeopardy" when program designers bring him a new application. If it takes too long to load, he kills it. It fails. But Google execs are not immune to failure. Google rejected more than a few programs after spending millions of dollars and hundreds of hours developing them. (PC magazine has a list of the top ten Google failures at www.pcworld.com/article/146101.)

The point is that successful companies are not afraid to fail. If you suffer from a fear of failure you probably will not succeed. Actually, you will probably fail. This thinking also leads to the dreaded disease called the paralysis of analysis. You can research an idea to death when you might just be better off giving your idea a shot and see if it works. If it doesn't, get through the learning experience quickly. Of course, sometimes an idea takes time to gel, so if you try something and it isn't working as fast as you had hoped it would, you need to ask yourself these questions: 1) Am I are heading in the right direction and just need to keep going? or, 2) Do I adjust what I'm doing rather than killing the concept? Often, you just have to keep plugging along until your product or service gains critical mass.

Fear of People does not really mean you are hiding in your house avoiding contact with others. Most folks who are afraid of people are afraid of being told "no." They use the excuse that they really don't want to bother anybody. If you have a product or service that folks really need and want, how are you bothering them by helping them get what they need? As a salesman, I know that everyone is not going to tell me yes when I offer them an opportunity. It is usually more stressful on the person saying no then on me because I don't take rejection personally. If I'm offering them the greatest thing since sliced bread and they don't want it, it is their loss, not mine.

Speaking of sliced bread, in 1912, Otto Frederick Rohwedder, from Davenport, Iowa, invented the Rohwedder Bread Slicer. Bakers were reluctant to pre-slice their bread as they worried the slices would go stale quicker. Mr. Rohwedder persisted, including attempting to keep the slices held together with hat pins, which didn't quite work out. It was not until 1928, when he enhanced his slicer with a wax paper wrapping system and found a baker by the name of Frank Bench in Missouri who was willing to give it a try that his idea took off. On July 7, 1928, the first loaves of Sliced Kleen Maid Bread hit the shelves and sales took off. In 1930, Wonder Bread hit the stores and the rest is history.

The point is that even though it took Mr. Rohwedder 16 years and some failed adjustments, like hat pins, to make his program work, he knew his idea was a winner and if he had to go to another state and meet new people, he did it. No FoF, no FoP for Mr. Rohwedder.

Now I can remember when I was a kid, we had a single slice bread slicer because the Wonder Bread came in such thick slices that you could put it in this contraption and run a knife down the middle and make two slices to make a not so bread-laden sandwich. Eventually Wonder Bread caught on and made an adjustment to sell "thin-sliced" bread. Does that make it even greater than sliced bread?

CONSIDERATIONS

As one of the founders and an instructor for the Entrepreneurial Academy in North Port and Punta Gorda, and a former SCORE counselor, I'm often asked if now is a good time to start a new business.

When the economy is booming, new business start-ups are pretty much a dime a dozen, and some of them even make it. In an average year, more than 500,000 new businesses are launched, and this year is no exception. In the first six months of 2010, Sarasota and Charlotte counties had more than 2,000 companies register as new ventures. Thousands more started home-based businesses such as multi-level marketing programs or services such as bookkeeping.

Of course, back in the boom times, it was easier to get funding for a new business. But Americans have an entrepreneurial spirit, and prognosticators of gloom and doom can't kill the American Dream.

Now is as good a time as any to get to work to make a dream a reality, though new business owners may need to be more creative in getting it off the ground and running.

Uncle Sugar may not want to throw money at your great idea, and the chances of getting a grant for a start up are slim. On the other hand, there are some opportunities you might be able to take advantage of, depending on the nature of your business so don't rule them out, just don't hold your breath waiting for the check to arrive.

Most small business start-ups I've seen lately start with what they have or get support from friends and family.

Some unemployed people who can't find a job in their profession start over and go into business for themselves.

Others see a need and get their business started based on opportunity.

And some start a business on a part time basis while working a job.

The key to success in any business start-up is planning. We've had several graduates of the Entrepreneurial Academy do the market research and discover that the chosen business is not going to work. It is much better to find out beforehand that an idea won't fly.

GETTING PAST THE GATEKEEPER

There is a little part of your brain known as your Reticular Activating System, or RAS, that acts as the gatekeeper of the mind. It filters what your mind accepts as fact or fiction or worthy of focus or distraction. It is the link between your conscious and subconscious. It is the "servo-mechanism" that Dr. Maxwell Maltz referred to in his 1960 book "Psycho-Cybernetics."

When I was growing up in Bethesda, Md., jet aircraft would, on a regular basis follow a low flight pattern over our house. They were pretty noisy and on occasion would rattle the house. After awhile we didn't notice the noise and rattling. Visitors would comment, and only then did we notice it. The RAS had deemed it a simple distraction and screened it out.

Over the years, you have programmed your comfort zone into your gatekeeper, who fights hard to keep you in the zone. If you have a dream outside your existing comfort zone, your RAS will kick in to remind you don't really want to stretch beyond your boundaries.

To get beyond your inner gatekeeper (or as I like to call it, out of your RAS), you need to do some reprogramming. One method is called Neurolinquistic Programming, or NLP. Another term for this is self talk. NLP was developed from the study of successful people. Their actions and the words they used were studied and used as a basis for helping others reprogram themselves.

When our goals exceed our comfort levels we step out on faith. Having faith is the first part of a three-part equation. So having faith in ourselves and our dreams is one-third of the way to success.

Next is formulating a plan to achieve success, much easier said than done. Focusing on your how is a stumbling block that keeps many a dreamer from taking a first step toward a dream. But if your faith, your why, is stronger than the gatekeeper's influence and your can focus on how to get what you want outside your comfort zone, you are 66 percent of the way home.

The third step is effort and if you have made it this far, you are two thirds of the way toward your dream, but you have to make the effort. Your RAS will be doing everything it can to talk you out of moving forward at this point. It is in its comfort zone and doesn't take kindly to being disturbed and all the NLP in the world will not overcome a lack of movement.

Faith x Focus x Effort = Success

As in any equation, a zero in any of the factors produces a zero result. All the focus and effort in the world without faith and belief in yourself and your dream will not produce the results you claim to want to accomplish.

I can't tell you how many small business owners I've talked to who are just waiting for snowbirds to arrive, bearing great quantities of cash. I've heard that regionally, the local population increases by about 20 percent "in season."

If you are offering goods and services and can't prosper with the existing 80 percent and see the additional 20 percent as gravy, you might need to rethink your business plan.

In his book <u>Jack, Straight from the Gut</u>, Jack Welch, former chairman of General Electric says, "When the rate of change inside an institution becomes slower than the rate of change outside, the end is in sight. The only question is when."

Mr. Welch also says, "There are no modest revolutions."

Change is tough, but we live in a world of change. Social networking, texting and smart phones have put a whole new face on marketing. If your business is not adapting and at a rapid pace, outside your comfort zone, failure is not an option, it is inevitable. You may just need to get your head out of your RAS!

QUICK RESPONSE

Have you seen those new Quick Response (QR) codes that are starting to show up all over the place? They are those square barcode things that you can hold up your smart phone to and it takes you to a website on your phone. They are popping up on ads in publications, on products in stores, on business cards, even on television. I read an article the other day that said that in Japan they put them on people's tombs and a click on them gives you a history of the person in the grave.

Both of my daughters who are in their 30's have Droid smart phones which I lovingly call "Pocket Rockets" that can do everything I can do on my laptop plus take pictures! I, on the other hand, am the proud owner of a stupid cell phone that works like a phone (OK, it does texting too, grudgingly). But I have to admit the day is coming when I'm going to have to upgrade if only to be able to play Angry Birds on my phone.

One of the things we teach our Entrepreneurial Academy students is to do is a PEST analysis. PEST is an acronym for Political, Economic, Social and Technological that focuses on the outside influences that can affect your business. The speed of technological change is simply amazing and not staying on top of it as a business owner is a huge mistake.

There is now a program called Square (www.squareup.com) that you can use to swipe debit and credit cards using your smart phone. If you deal with customers outside your place of business this can be a great tool to collect payments instantly.

I had a friend tell me the other day that he uses his I-phone now for everything and doesn't even use a laptop in his office. Which means that customers know they can get a hold of him at any time by phone or text as long as he has his cell phone handy. He can download entire documents in his phone and respond instantly to customer requests.

So what does all this mean for small businesses? I remember when computers became a "must have" for business as it would increase the speed of doing business. Seemed to me it just added more work, learning how to use all the various business programs, but it did speed things up which also seemed to add to the workload. Now the functions of computers have leaped into our cell phones. There is no escape! If you are a sole proprietor you now have no place to hide. And while the access to customers and customers' access to you is certainly enhanced it can be a distraction when you are trying to get something else done.

Another friend, whose work is on a computer, said she is constantly distracted from doing her job as emails, instant messaging, text messages, and tweets are constantly arriving in addition to telephone calls. Of course she also has to keep up on FaceBook and other social media while all this is going on.

According to a recent study by AT&T (http://smallbusiness.foxbusiness.com/technology-web/2011/03/15/small- business-social-media-wireless-technology/) 96% of small businesses are using wireless technology in some form in their business. In addition 72% of small businesses reported using mobile apps in their business and 41% have a FaceBook business page.

So is all this stuff a blessing or a curse? I have no answer to that but I do know new apps are appearing every day and if they can be used to improve your business your customers will be expecting you to use them. The speed of information exchange is literally changing the way we do business. You need to stay up to speed.

POCKET ROCKETS

In 1943 the US Military commissioned John Mauchly and John Eckert to develop a computer that could compute better telemetry for cannons. The feds put up a half million dollars and after a year of design and another 18 months to build it the Electrical Numerical Integrator And Calculator (ENIAC) was born.

The first super computer, ENIAC, contained 17,468 vacuum tubes along with 70,000 resistors, 10,000 capacitors, 1,500 relays, 6,000 manual switches and 5 million soldered joints. It covered 1800 square feet of floor space, weighed 30 tons, and consumed 160 kilowatts of electrical power. It was so large that folks on roller skates would roll around inside replacing the tubes to keep it operating.

Eventually ENIAC became BINAC which used magnetic tapes to store data and the company the two Johns started was purchased by Remington Rand Corporation and became UNIVAC. My first introduction to computing was on a UNIVAC machine that you had to program with punch cards.

When Tom Watson, then Chairman of IBM, said in 1958: "I think there is a world market for about five computers," he was obviously wrong. Today over half of all cell phones are smartphones with computing power far beyond the imaginations of the founders of ENIAC.

These smartphones, or as I call them, "pocket rockets" are changing the way we live. From texting to tweeting, and video on YouTube, we have gone from 24 hour news shows to 24 hours of not having a private life. Folks are posting their pictures and messages on FaceBook from their iphones and droids 24/7 these days.

While it has certainly had an effect on the news media, more folks are getting their news off a computer these days, it also is having an effect on customer service. Customers are coming to expect immediate responses to their queries.

Customer expectations are why you can now track a package sent through UPS anywhere in the world on your smartphone. It has gotten to the point that Ashton Kutcher just hired a firm to handle his Twitter account with over 8 million followers. It seems, according to ShowBizSpy.com, he tweeted his outrage over the firing of Joe Paterno until he was swamped with outraged followers who pointed out the connection to child molestation. He was forced to delete his tweet and turn the whole thing over to his production company to handle.

It is not just customer expectations over the speed of transactions it also includes your whole company image. The website, Yelp.com, is about to go public following the success of Groupon. Yelp is a site where anybody with a customer complaint can post it about you instantly. You, as a business, have an opportunity to refute the complaint or make good on it and post it. However unless you are monitoring what is said about your business on the web, you might not even know you were being publicly slammed.

Had one too many at the office Christmas party? The pictures taken by anybody with a smartphone in their pocket are going to look great on facebook. Yeah right. In this day of instant messaging your personal as well as corporate life are an open book and you need to be ready to handle it.

Here's another consideration, you may have spent big bucks to put up a snappy website and posted QR codes on all your printed materials so folks can find it with their smartphone apps. Have you checked your site on a pocket rocket? The big screen does not always translate well to the small screen on a phone. You do need a website as more folks are going online to get information, but you had better make sure your site does what you want it to do on all available media.

We have come a long way technology wise from ENIAC to the iPhone. We need to be prepared to deal with it. I told Annie at Seeport Optometry that one of the consequences of all these folks staring at small screens for long periods of time was going to be a boon to the optometrists.

FUSION MARKETING

The best marketing you can get is word of mouth. That's it. End of article. OK, not really. The point is your business can be made or broken by what other people say about you.

Jay Levinson, of Guerilla Marketing fame, is a big fan of fusion marketing. Another term for it is strategic alliances, but what it all amounts to is word of mouth marketing. If you own a business and do a great job for a customer and you notice they have other needs and you refer them to somebody you know who can also meet their needs and also do a great job for them, you are doing the customer and a business partner both a service.

In the grand scheme of things and the karma of life it is the building block of success to get referrals. I was chatting the other night with Bill Ginn of Presto Air about who refers him and who he refers customers to and how important it is that they do a great job at what they do. He can be the best in the business and suggest somebody to his customers who does a shoddy job and it will reflect on him. On the other hand, a customer who get's great service from a referral will be a customer for life of his service and refer him to their friends. That's the way word of mouth advertising works.

My company is a member of three Chambers of Commerce locally. We are active participants in all of them because we are always looking for folks we can partner with and who support what we do. We, in turn, refer folks to fellow Chamber members when we meet people who need their services. We can refer them because we know that they are not only sound business people but active in their community.

People like to do business with people they like, it's that simple. If you can be pleasant as well as a master of what you do, you are more than welcomed to be my partner in our efforts in restoring the American Dream. Yeah, I know, that's a darned huge vision but like somebody once said if you reach for the stars and only make it to the moon you are way ahead of the game.

Fusion marketing is developing partnerships. Synergy is when the sum of the parts is greater than the whole. A great strategic alliance is when you do your best and you are able to gain the trust of your customer and refer them to somebody who does their best and makes you look good in the process. It is the ultimate win-win situation.

Who can you team up with to spread the word of your great services? Who are you willing to give a referral to your clients? Who do you want on your referral team? It can make or break your business.

EMAIL MARKETING

I just got an email from Jay Levinson of Guerrilla Marketing talking about email marketing. I was a little surprised that I got it on a Sunday when the purpose of the email was to tell folks that the absolute best day to send an email to prospective customers is on Friday. I don't know how he got his statistics, but he claims that emails sent on a Friday get 23 percent more sales.

In addition, he suggests that Wednesday is the worst day of the week to send email solicitations and Tuesday is the worst day to get actual views. On the other hand, he says that Thursday emails will get the most views.

Several years ago, I started working with Diane Caputo at Old Monty's in Punta Gorda as a SCORE counselor. One of the first things we did was to map out a marketing calendar for the year. We developed a comment card that requested an email address to add to her mailing list. Then, the first of every month, we began an email marketing campaign.

Ms. Caputo will tell you that she had her doubts about doing the e-mail campaign. The first email she sent out contained a special that required receivers to print the mail and bring it in to take advantage of the monthly special. Fifty of her customers printed the email and brought it in to take advantage of the deal that first month. Their average bill was around $30. One email generated $1,500 in business. To this day, I get an email the first of the month from Ms. Caputo with a new creative special for her customers.

The basis of Guerrilla Marketing is using your time and talent to market — and saving your treasure. Email marketing is a major inexpensive tool that most any business can add to its tool belt. Yet most businesses miss out on this opportunity. I'm no fan of spam, but when folks opt in to your mailing list, it is not only not spam, but if your email is not intrusive and boring, it is welcomed.

One of the best email marketers in the area is Mark Asciutto, owner of Visani Comedy Zone. Mr. Asciutto has comment cards on every table and his servers promote using them for a drawing each night for tickets to a future show. The first time I filled one out, by the time I got home that night I had an email from Mr. Asciutto, thanking me for coming and telling me about next week's show. Pretty impressive.

The more personal your email, the more powerful the message. Ms. Caputo often talks about her family in her monthly emails as well as offering a monthly special. She has been in business for more than 28 years and her kids grew up in the business. That personal touch makes her emails more than a sales pitch. She often gets responses from her snowbird customers letting her know they are on their way back.

I get more than my share of junk email, and mostly, I just delete it. The frequency of your messages can turn off your audience. More than once a month is probably a waste of time. But Mr. Asciutto, on the other hand, has new talent arriving each week so a weekly blast is not out of the question.

Don't forget to include a link to your website in your email. A special offer gives incentive for customers to visit your website.

If you are using a service such as Constant Contact, be aware that you must get permission to use an email address. They will cut you off if they get spam complaints from folks on your list. Many email servers also limit the number of emails you can send in a day, so if you are sending emails directly, you could get a 24-hour cutoff in your service if you send out too many. And many spam filters detect emails with multiple addresses and send it directly to the junk file.

The point is that email marketing can be a great tool if done right. So start collecting those email addresses and stay in contact.

DIFFUSION OF INNOVATION

The theory of diffusion of innovation was first proposed by French sociologist, Gabriel Tarde in 1890. It suggests how new ideas and products, over time, are adopted by successive groups of consumers.

The first group to adopt a new product, service, or idea, are innovators who account for about 2.5% of the market for the new innovation. These are the folks who camp out to be first in line to buy the latest in technology. They are risk takers.

The second group, early adopters, make up 13.5% of the market. They have a high degree of opinion leadership among market segments but are more discrete in making choices. These first two groups are often called the "low hanging fruit" in marketing.

Once these groups have accepted the innovation the early majority kicks in who represent 34% of the market. When they start buying, sales take off.

Next come the late majority at 34% also of the market. They tend to be skeptical of innovation and only come on board when innovation is trending toward the norm.

The last 16% are laggards who tend to be traditionalists with an aversion to change.

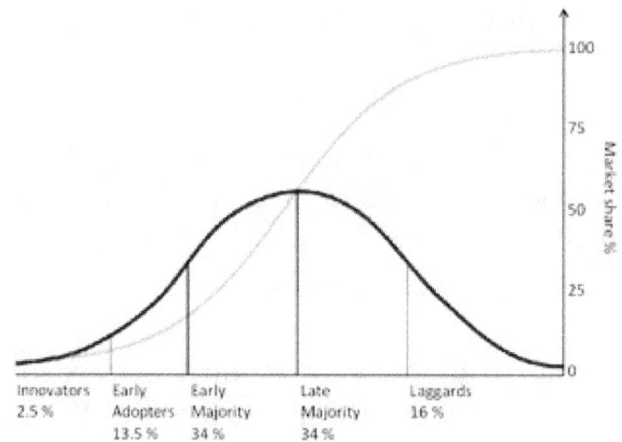

What this all means to small business start-ups and those introducing innovative new products and services is that you need to break through that first 16% of your target market for your innovative idea to get traction with the masses. This is called critical mass in the market place of ideas.

Critical mass is the point in the adoption curve when continued adoption is self sustaining because enough individuals have come on board and word of mouth kicks in among social networks.

There have always been social networks long before Facebook. Whether they were called tribes, kingdoms, countries, families, cliques, or just friends, they have always been a part of social existence. The only thing that has changed is the speed and reach of social interaction. Now, with the click of a keyboard or touch pad, opinion leaders can share their preferences, good or bad, with millions of viewers. A "tweet" can make or break a market. A funny email or interesting YouTube video can go viral and travel around the globe in the blink of an eye.

What, for some innovations, took years to reach critical mass can now happen overnight. For example, King Camp Gillette invented the idea of a safety razor with disposable blades in 1895. It took him six years to get it developed and it finally received a patent in 1904. While this high end product received some minimal traction, it was not until world war one that his innovation really took off with the sale of 3.5 million razors and 35 million blades to the US military.

On the other hand, Rovio Company, that introduced the phone app "Angry Birds" has already sold over 10 million downloads at 99 cents each and has signed a deal with 20th Century Fox to develop movies, TV shows, and comic books to extend the brand.

The key for the acceptance of any new idea is reaching critical mass in target markets. Whether that takes 19 years as in the case of Gillette or 19 weeks for an internet game, the dedicated entrepreneur has to have the personality traits I discussed previously (passion, purpose, perspective, persistence, and personality) and the financial means to hang in there until that point is reached.

OUTSTANDING CUSTOMER SERVICE

According to Customer Service Magazine, providing outstanding customer service for your products and services give you the following:

• Increased customer satisfaction

• Increased revenues

• Increased repeat and referral customer traffic

• Less employee turnover

• Increased profits

For years companies treated customer service as a euphemism for the old "complaint department". When a customer had a problem he or she would be tossed into the limbo of customer service. The sad part of that equation was they usually ended up with poor service and excuses rather than solutions to their problems.

Now I'm aware that you can't solve everyone's problems and that sometimes things don't go the way they are supposed to, but that is no excuse and you can bet you are going to lose customers. Outstanding customer service is simply delivering over and above customers' expectations. Or, as my Dad always used to say, "Results, not excuses".

Ordinary businesses do things ordinarily. Extraordinary businesses exceed expectations. They literally deliver on their promises and then some.

Of course there are folks that you never make happy for one reason or another. But your willingness to try in most cases can make a big difference. A friend told me the other day that at an Applebees in Kentucky when the manager receives a complaint from a customer the next day the manager would show up at the complainer's house with a dozen roses and an apology. But not just an apology, he would thank them for pointing out a problem and ask them for the opportunity to come back and give him the chance to make it right. The place always has waiting lines to get in.

Probably the premier company at practicing outstanding customer service is the Ritz Carlton Hotel chain. While the architecture of each property in any part of the world attempts to adapt to the flavor of the area, the persistent devotion to "wow" their guests never changes. It begins in their hiring practices. Ritz doesn't hire employees, they select team members. The motto of all team members is "We are ladies and gentlemen serving ladies and gentlemen." Even new hires can spend up to $2,000 of the hotel's money if need be to quickly solve any problem a guest may have. Any team member is empowered to be a problem solver and if they hear of a problem they own it and are responsible for solving it. The company posts on their website:

(http://corporate.ritzcarlton.com/en/About/GoldStandards. htm) their "Gold Standards" and at the beginning of each shift, team members in each department review them and discuss them. They have estimated that the average customer over the course of their lifetime will spend over $250,000 utilizing their services which include in addition to great hotel rooms, world class spas, restaurants, gift shops, and several golf courses.

In addition, if you have ever been a Ritz guest, they keep a permanent file on you in their worldwide computer system so the next time you visit they can be ready with all of your needs. Want a cold bottle of beer and a dish of peanuts when you arrive? It will be ready and waiting when you check into your room on your next visit without even having to ask. On their gold standards web site they list the following service values:

1. I build strong relationships and create Ritz-Carlton guests for life.

2. I am always responsive to the expressed and unexpressed wishes and needs of our guests.

3. I am empowered to create unique, memorable and personal experiences for our guests.

4. I understand my role in achieving the Key Success Factors, embracing Community Footprints and creating The Ritz-Carlton Mystique.

5. I continuously seek opportunities to innovate and improve The Ritz-Carlton experience.

6. I own and immediately resolve guest problems.

7. I create a work environment of teamwork and lateral service so that the needs of our guests and each other are met.

8. I have the opportunity to continuously learn and grow.

9. I am involved in the planning of the work that affects me.

10. I am proud of my professional appearance, language and behavior.

11. I protect the privacy and security of our guests, my fellow employees and the company's confidential information and assets.

12. I am responsible for uncompromising levels of cleanliness and creating a safe and accident-free environment.

Outstanding customer service is what your customers expect. Can you deliver?

SMILE

Earlier we discussed Customer Service and the
training programs of the Ritz Carlton Hotels. A key
point in the article was that whoever on staff hears about
a customer problem owns it. Everyone on staff is in
customer service.

Does everyone on your team have training in how to
handle customer problems and complaints?
Do they know how to handle an irate customer?
Do they know what to do with the person who behaves
like the south end on a northbound horse?

Most folks who have a problem have a legitimate need
that should be immediately addressed. People who have
a situation with your products or services can be a great
source of information about something that may need
to be corrected in your system. They really can help you
to improve and avoid future problems that you may not
have been aware of until somebody points it out.

If you have a system in place to solve their problem to
their satisfaction, on the spot, 90% of them will continue
to do business with you. If a solution takes a little more
time to resolve, or has to be passed off up the food chain
to somebody with more authority, even if it gets

resolved in the customer's favor, you will only retain 70% as customers. It costs you 20% in repeat business by not having a system in place to resolve problems immediately. If that means that you have to give your staff problem solving authority and will back them up both mentally and financially, it will make you money in the long run.

Ritz gives even their newest employees up to $2,000 in backing to solve customer problems. They have run the numbers and they know that over the life of an average customer repeat business is worth $250,000 per customer. Sounds like a no brainer to me.

Now I'm guessing that most small businesses have no idea what the value of long term repeat customers are worth to them. Not just in terms of positive word of mouth advertising, but actual cash in their pockets over the life of the relationship. For example, let's say you own a restaurant and your average customer comes in twice a month and spends $20 per visit. That's $40 a month or $480 a year. Spread that out over ten years and you are talking some serious income. Multiply that by 100 customers and you begin to get the point.

And here's another point, it costs 6 times more to get new customers than it does to keep the ones you have happy. It costs you one sixth as much to keep your happy customers. And they tell their friends. Not a bad deal.

But, into each life some rain must fall and at some point you are going to have to deal with that southern end of the horse who likes to complain and does so, shall we say, unpleasantly. And we all have seen it or done it. Yes I know you love your business and your first impulse is to defend your policies and your pride. There's an old saying that goes, "when you wrestle with a pig, you both get muddy and the pig likes it."

So how do you deal with the irate person spitting bullets in your face? First you listen. You let them vent. Hey, to be honest, maybe you had it coming. Don't get defensive. Listen with empathy and try to discern what the facts are in the situation. Solve their problem to the best of your ability, maybe even above and beyond their expectations. As Michael LeBoeuf says in his great book, How to Win Customers and Keep Them for Life: "A customer with the passion to get angry also has the ability to be loyal. Remember it is the nice customers who quietly walk away and don't come back that do the most damage."

He makes the point that only 4% of dissatisfied customers ever say anything. They just walk away and don't come back and they tell their friends about their problems they had with your service. I've been told that the opposite of love is not hate, it is indifference. Folks have to care about you enough to get mad at you. If they don't care they ignore you.

Yes, you can't win them all and frankly some of them are not worth winning. If there is nothing you can do to calm an irate customer down, then simply thank them for their opinion, give them a refund if they deserve it, and fire them as a customer. Some folks just like to argue. They are a minority, but they exist. Wish them well and wish them away and move on.

As Elliott Hubbard put it, "Every man is a damn fool for at least five minutes out of every day. Wisdom consists of not exceeding the limit."

SELLING

Recently, in a sales training program I was doing, I asked for a show of hands of anybody in the class who was not in sales. One guy in the back of the room raised his hand. I asked him if he was married. Based on his affirmative answer I asked if his wife was a mail-order bride or was there some selling involved in convincing her to marry him. He got my point…we are all in sales at some point in our lives. From our first effort to convince Mom to buy us that candy bar in the grocery checkout line, we are selling.

So why is sales such a stressful situation for most people if we do it all the time? Probably the biggest fear folks have about selling is fear of rejection.

Nobody likes to be told NO! The other side of that coin is that most folks also don't like to tell anybody NO! Dale Carnegie summed it up in his book <u>How to Win Friends and Influence People</u> by stating:

"When a person says "no" and really means it he is doing far more than saying a word of two letters. His entire organism gathers itself together into a condition of rejection. There is, usually in minute but sometimes observable, physical withdrawal or readiness for withdrawal. The whole neuro-muscular system, in short,

sets itself on guard against acceptance. Where a person says "yes" none of the withdrawing activities take place. The organism is in a forward-moving, accepting open attitude."

The fact is people like to buy stuff (say yes) they just don't like to be sold. As Carnegie points out:

"Those convinced against their will
Are of the same opinion still".

Good salespeople have several things in common but the most important skills they bring to the table are listening and observing. I've had sales managers tell me many times, "It's a numbers game. The more people you call on the more sales you make." Sure that is true. However we are all limited by the same 24 hours in a day and the time devoted to playing the numbers can be incredibly wasted calling on folks who have no need or interest in what you have to offer. And, racking up the rejections may indeed lead you to a sale or two but at what cost to you in terms of your personal return on investment.

Even professional salespeople tell me the one thing they hate to do is "cold calling". Honestly I wish most of them wouldn't do it the way they do it and give the rest of us a bad name. The purpose of a cold call is not to make a sale. The purpose of a cold call is to determine first who is the decision maker and if they might have a need for what you have to offer and second is to make an appointment to come back and visit with them when you can discuss how your offering can meet their needs.

Sales Statistics: 48% of sales people never follow up with a prospect. 25% of sales people make a second contact and stop. 12% of sales people only make three contacts and stop. Only 10% of sales people make more than three contacts.

2% of sales are made on the first contact. 3% of sales are made on the second contact. 5% of sales are made on the third contact. 10% of sales are made on the fourth contact. 80% of sales are made on the fifth to twelfth contact.

The reason that 80% of sales are made on the 5th to the 12th sales call is that it takes time to develop a relationship where you are meeting the needs of a potential client. The way you determine their needs is by listening and observing. There's an old saying in sales that Samson slew 40,000 Philistines with the jawbone of an ass and every day salespeople do the same thing by talking too much. Market research is nothing more than listening and observing and testing what people need. Sales is simply matching the needs with the needy.

And what determines need? Most psychologists will tell you that the top motivators are pleasure and pain. We seek to enhance our pleasure and avoid pain.

According to the book, <u>Winning Strategies in Selling</u> by Kinder, Kinder, & Staubach, there are six basic motives which move folks to buy. They are:

- Desire for money gain (profit)
- Fear of loss (security)
- Pride of ownership (status)
- Interest in doing it easier (efficiency)
- Desire for excitement (pleasure)
- Interest in self improvement (effectiveness)

Meet their needs and they want to buy. No selling required!

IN or ON

I'm a great fan of Michael Gerber and his E-Myth books. He talks about working ON your business as opposed to working IN your business. Yes, I know, you know how to do what you do and you know how better than anybody else. The problem is, you only have the same 24 hours in a day we all do and your technical skills will only bring you so much per hour of time invested. You are trading hours for dollars.

You can invest your time in performing your technical skill or expanding the utilization of your skill set. That's the trade off. Let me put it in simple terms. Let's say you are a great painter and you have a room to paint. Somebody is willing to pay you $15 an hour to paint the room. It will take you 3 hours to paint that room if you do it yourself and you pocket the whole 45 bucks from the deal.
However you could train another person to do the job and pay them $8 an hour to do it. They don't have your technical skills so it will take them 4 hours to do the job. You quoted the job at $45. The job gets done and you pay your apprentice $32 and put $13 in your pocket.

The difference between the technician and the business leader is the technician wants the whole $45 bucks for the gig and ignores the fact they just freed up 3 hours of time to do something else (they could have been painting another room and spent an hour working on finding more rooms to paint, pocketed $58, and built a backlog of new orders for more painting jobs). Yes, he only got paid $13 rather than $15 for the fourth hour when he could have been painting rather than selling his services and building a backlog of orders. Or, he could have been paid nothing for his selling time and only collected on his technical production time.

That's the difference in working ON rather than IN your business. Either you can do it yourself (IN) or teach somebody else your method of doing things (ON). I've heard it said it takes 10,000 hours of practice to master a skill. As a skilled technician you may well have taken those hours to master your craft. But I don't care what your trade is or your skill at doing it is, if you only get paid for the time you do it, you are trading hours for dollars and I don't care who you are, you only get 24 each day.

By hiring an apprentice or another skilled technician to do something you don't have time to do because you are busy building your business (bookkeeping comes to mind) you free up your time to be a business leader and work ON your business. Yes, you do need to practice your craft but you can't do it by yourself.

When you open a business, you have made the decision to quit being the technician and become the business leader. There is a huge difference in the skills required to be a hairdresser and the skills necessary to run a successful hair salon or to be a great chef and own a successful restaurant or even a great dentist to run a successful dental practice.

(I can't tell you the number of hours I've sat reading 3 month old magazines in dental waiting rooms... customer service is apparently not a required course in dental school).

You start each day with 24 hours (Time) and the skills you have chosen to accumulate over time (Talent) and a few bucks in your pocket (Treasure). You can only increase your time by hiring others to do what you do, or don't want to do, or don't have the skills to do (yes, I do have an MBA and I still don't want to do bookkeeping). You can only increase your talent by experience or through other peoples' experience (OPE) and it can be a whole lot cheaper to learn from OPE than to lose your shirt in the process of gaining your own experience (yes, Dad, I hear you "some will learn no other way").

You can increase your treasure by trading hours for dollars or trading dollars for hours of other's time and talent. The difference between IN and ON.

IN or ON part 2

OK,OK, I get it. It is danged hard when you are a one person business not to be constantly working IN your business. If you don't do it who will? On the other hand if you are not working ON your business how in the heck will you ever be able to grow your business into a world class company? Unless you are constantly innovating, quantifying, and orchestrating your business you are once again just trading hours for dollars as a technician. In other words your business is running you instead of you running your business.

Yes, you do need to work IN your business to generate funds. You provide the goods and services that your customers need. I don't expect young entrepreneurs to understand all the ins and outs of management and marketing. We now supply our Entrepreneurial Academy students with a copy of Michael Gerber's <u>E-Myth Revisited</u>. There are no tests in our class and no required reading assignments. We handed out the book in our last class and after a couple of weeks I asked the class how many had started reading it. About 5 people raised their hands and all of them praised the book. It reads like a novel not a text book, but it conveys tons of wisdom.

I gave a copy to a friend who owns a business and she said she didn't have time to read she was just too busy. I

gave it to her anyway and told her when she had a moment just read a couple of pages (ok I suggested she put it in the porcelain reading room next to the throne if you get my drift). She got started and could not put it down.
Just the simple fact of reading a book that can help you improve the way you do business is working ON your business.

Creativity is essentially new ideas. Innovation is new ideas in action. Do all innovative ideas work? Nope, that's why you need to test and quantify the results of your innovations. For example, Gerber suggests to a client that he try dressing all the employees in his retail shop in brown for 3 weeks and quantify everything that occurs for the time period (number of customers, time spent in the store, dollar amount of purchases, etc). The next 3 weeks he dressed all his employees in dark blue suits with white shirts and ties with a little red in them (see John Molloy's book Dress for Success) and again kept track of the statistics. The second 3 weeks produced an increase in sales of over 10%. That simple innovation changed the bottom line of the company for the good.
A dress code was added to the employee manual (orchestration).

Now, don't get me wrong. You and I have dealt with folks who have provided poor customer service with the saying, "That's company policy". Well my personal policy is not to do business with you and your policies. Everyone who works for your company is in sales, like it or lump it. The purpose of orchestration is not to put your people in a box. The purpose of having a company policy is to provide

consistent quality products and services. It costs 6 times as much to get a new customer as it does to keep an existing customer and have them keep coming back. So the number one policy in any business should be outstanding customer service.
All the demographics and psycho graphics in the world don't amount to a hill of beans in a one on one situation with a customer or a prospective customer. Their perception is their reality. Your job is to meet their needs. Those who deliver above and beyond expectations are the people who succeed.

An old saying is that if you do good, folks will tell 2 people (word of mouth advertising) however if you treat someone poorly they will tell 10 people. I've got news for you, it you treat somebody poorly they will tell 10,000 people on Facebook, or Yelp, or Twitter, or Angie's List (just to name a few). But that goes both ways, now if you WOW somebody with great service they will tell their Facebook friends or Tweet something nice about you.

Your job as a business leader is to provide that WOW to everyone you deal with. That WOW is the innovative unexpected service you provide. T. Scott Gross has a couple of great books on Outrageous Customer Service.
He took a chicken franchise to number one in the chain by hiring great people and giving them the opportunity to be creative and innovate. Folks would line up outside his door to take advantage of his "Cackle Like a Chicken" discounts where he would knock a buck off your lunch if you would do your best chicken imitation. Crazy? Unexpected? Innovative? You bet, and it worked.

What can you do that your customers would appreciate that differentiates you from the competition? Your unique selling proposition is the service you provide. Innovating, quantifying, and orchestrating that into your business is working ON your business.

JUST DO IT…NOW

According to Michael Gerber, author and founder of a business skills training company, in a recent E-Myth e-mail, there are seven reasons that we procrastinate:

1. You are feeling overwhelmed by a particular task.

2. You are afraid that you will fail.

3. You feel unwilling or unable to make a decision.

4. You are overworked or too tired.

5. You just don't want to do it.

6. You are too disorganized and distracted to effectively budget the time.

7. You don't want to commit to starting a task unless you know it will be perfect.

Talking to a friend of mine back in my old days as an association manager in Washington, D.C., he told me he procrastinated on purpose on some occasions. He said that after being on the job for many years and having to often do the same thing over and over again, he sometimes put things off to the last minute just to see if he could get it done right before the whistle blew and time ran out. He reported that it made repeated mundane tasks a little more exciting and besides it saved him time, as he had to get the job done in less time. I guess there was some thrill in the sense that if he didn't get the job done he might get fired. After thinking about it I had to agree that sometimes I did that too. I don't recommend it. A looming deadline can also be pretty stressful when your job is on the line.

Every year, before we made out our annual budget for the next year, I would take my staff out of town for a weekend retreat. We spent the weekend with a calendar and several flip charts, mapping out a program of work for the coming year. We had a page for each month and what needed to be done that month and assigned the task to the person in charge of getting it done. Once we mapped out the entire year, we started to put a price tag on each event to develop the year's budget. Essentially what we put together was an annual "To-Do" list.

With everyone understanding what needed to be done and who was supposed to do it some interesting things started to happen. Many items that could be put off until the following month started to get done a month early. Because there was no pressure, the work started to keep being cranked out earlier and earlier. We posted the program of work on the bulletin board and as each task was completed a check mark was put next to the task.

There was always some satisfaction in filling in the checks. And if somebody had not completed their task and the deadline was looming, we could offer to assist them in getting their work done.

I just finished listening to a book called <u>Focus</u> by the Franklin/Covey group that originated the Day Timer program. One of the things they suggest to do is to not only do a daily to-do list but to rank all the tasks of the day according to urgency and importance. All of the important tasks are "A" tasks. Less important tasks are "B" tasks and those that need to be done but are not of high importance get a "C" rating. Then each of the categories are ranked based on the urgency of the task such as A1, A2, A3, and B1, B2, on down the list. (If all of your tasks for the day are all A1's, then you are either running a hospital emergency room on New Year's Eve or headed for burnout.) You then start at A1 and work your way through the list. They also suggest that you put the task that is giving you the most consternation and possibly causing you to procrastinate at the top of your list. That way you can check it off your list and move on without the pressure.

So to quote Larry the Cable Guy, just "Get 'er done!"

"Knowledge without action becomes trivia"
– Brendon Sommers

IT'S JUST BUSINESS

Abe Vigoda, who played "Fish" in the Barney Miller TV series, also played an underboss in the Corleone Family in the Godfather movies. When confronted by Michael Corleone for selling out the family he says, "It was nothing personal, Michael. Just Business."

I'm amazed sometimes at the creativity of folks who throw roadblocks in the way of small business owners and justify it as "just business". From blatant to sneaky and underhanded, competitors, government agencies, and folks who are just jealous of others' success find ways to make it harder for small businesses to succeed.

Governing bodies from agencies to professional societies pass rules and regulations under the egis of public good that over time become hoops that small business owners must jump through to practice their craft. Some are necessary to insure quality and public health. Some are just plain restrictive to keep out competition. Others are just dumb.

Our own small business was required by the purchasing department of a government body to buy fire insurance on City Hall to teach a class in the building. Now I could understand that if we were teaching a cooking class or advanced fire eating or model rocketry but not classes on how to start a successful business in a building next door to the fire department. But, that was required, and we have a policy.

There are many professions that require licensing and testing to be in business. Many are skilled positions that need special training. I have a family full of lawyers and I know the training they have to go through to pass the Bar exam. On the other hand I know many lawyers who did all the work, passed the Bar but do not practice their craft. My Dad was one of them.

I'm all for competition. It keeps the cost of goods in line in the market place. But I know from experience that some competitors don't play fair. Most small businesses operate on a local level. But even on a local level competition can be unfair. We have had folks, shall we say, tell untruths about us. And you know what, you just have to work your way through it and move on.

With all the new media available from sites like Yelp and Angie's List anyone, including your competitors, can post something negative about you or your business. There are public relations firms that do nothing but search out negative posts and apply counter measures. It literally has become an industry.

There is an old saying that those who stick their head above the crowd are going to catch a few tomatoes in the face. The greater your success in business the more you attract those tomatoes. The reality is it is a fact of life that somebody is going to pitch something rotten your way for whatever their reason and it is "just business".

You don't have to like it, you just have to deal with it. Focus on your dream and have faith in your abilities and keep moving forward. After all, it's just business.

RIDING THE ROLLER COASTER

At a recent Marketing Roundtable seminar, one of our partners, John Gulick, did a great job of demonstrating how to develop and cost out your annual budget for marketing your business. I was asked afterwards if there are any spreadsheets for developing an annual, month by month, business budget. The good news is that there are and they are free. You can go to www.score.org and click on the business tools section and download an excel spreadsheet that gives you a 12 month program to estimate your income and expenses for the year.

The spreadsheets force you to focus on each month individually and seriously think about the ebb and flow of your business model. In previous columns I've mentioned some of our Entrepreneurial Academy graduates who ran the numbers for their business ideas and realized before sinking their life savings into a new venture that no matter how great their idea was, the numbers just didn't work. Now entrepreneurs are an optimistic group in general (you really have to be), so I counsel students to go back after their first shot at this and run the numbers again in a "worst case scenario". Reality is, in all probability, somewhere in between the optimistic and pessimistic outcomes of the exercise.

It becomes pretty obvious in looking at somebody's numbers if they show a steady upward growth that they might be overlooking the business cycle in their estimations. Like I've said, you have to be a believer in yourself and your ideas to even open your doors, but it doesn't mean you have to be a damn fool in the process. Here in Southwest Florida, many businesses are affected by the seasons. If your business caters to "Snowbirds" you are kidding yourself if you think your business is going to continue to grow to new heights in June and July over say February. It ain't gonna happen! It happened just the other day in discussing a business plan with some folks who were sure their business was going to grow at a rate of about 5% each month. If 20% of the population splits town for the summer, who is going to take up the slack?

Many of our entrepreneurs are one person shops. For several years I had a management and marketing consulting business in Washington, DC. While the management side of the business was steady with annual contracts, the marketing side was a continuous roller coaster ride. When I was out selling, new business was coming in the door. When I was providing the services contracted with the new business I was, as a sole proprietor, obviously not out bringing in new business and when the projects were complete I was back out on the street selling again. That side of my business was always a cash flow consideration as money was going out while I was selling and nothing was coming in unless I was providing finished product. While I've always enjoyed riding on roller coasters, it is not so much fun in a business context.

The key to business budgeting is being honest with yourself. In the 30+ years I worked with trade and professional associations, each year I would have to make out a plan of work for the year and a budget to meet that plan of work. All of that had to go before an Executive Committee and a Board of Directors for approval. These were smart folks who had businesses of their own and could spot a weak plan in a heartbeat. Raises and bonuses, not to mention my continued employment, were based on how realistic and close I was in my estimations when my annual audit came back from our CPA.

Many folks who start new businesses have never had to deal with that type of situation. It is a reason many small businesses fail. Now I'll tell you a shocker, like it or not, you will probably be in business for yourself in the next 8 years. Last year Intuit published a report called Intuit 2020 which predicted 20 changes that will occur in the workplace in the current decade (http://about.intuit.com/futureofsmallbusiness/). Here's a quote from Trend 14 titled "Work Shifts from Full-Time to Free Agent Employment":

"Today, roughly 25 to 30 percent of the US workforce is contingent, and more than 80 percent of large corporations plan to substantially increase their use of a flexible workforce in the coming years."

The report goes on to state that by 2020 over 40% of the workforce will be contingent. Contingent is a nice way of saying you will be getting a 1099 instead of a W-2 at the end of the year. In other words, more and more folks will be independent contractors instead of employees. In case you have not been reading the news this is already happening in the workplace.

The era of YOU, Inc. is coming. You had better get ready. Hey, I'll even save you a seat on the roller coaster!

A UNIQUE SELLING PROPOSITION

Have you noticed that one of the strongest franchise operations in the world keeps reinventing itself? Why would you want to mess with success? I'm talking about McDonald's — and the old 15-cent hamburger stand ain't what it used to be!

Ray Kroc was selling milkshake machines in 1954 when he met up with the McDonald brothers who were running a hamburger stand in San Bernardino, Calif. He liked what he saw as well as saw the opportunity to sell a whole bunch of milkshake blenders, and convinced them to let him replicate their operation. The rest is history.

I'm old enough to remember when the first MickeyD's opened in Rockville, Md., and we drove the 15 miles or so to get those 15-cent hamburgers and fries at the golden arches. The menu options were pretty limited at that time: just burgers, fries, soft drinks and shakes. No McChicken, McRib, Fish Fillets, Happy Meals, McCoffees or Frapaccinos. Most of those were a long time in coming.

McDonald's is constantly trying new products to add to the menu. It consistently adapts its marketing strategies to meet changing tastes and market opportunities. Over the years, I've watched McDonald's go from the original Ronald McDonald (Willard Scott), to Mac Tonight and the Hamburgler. I've seen the company respond to heat from environmentalists and dump its Styrofoam containers for paper. I've even recently observed its response to the assault on fast food as the excuse for obesity with the addition of fruit, oatmeal and bottled water. The company is constantly adapting.

What has not changed at McDonald's is its unique selling proposition, or USP. Firmly implanted in the thick operation manuals and training programs McDonald's franchisees receive are four very important words that Mr. Kroc insisted on at all of his restaurants:

"If I had a brick for every time I've repeated the phrase 'Quality, Service, Cleanliness and Value,' I think I'd probably be able to bridge the Atlantic Ocean with them."

—Ray Kroc

Quality, Service, and Value are no-brainers when it comes to developing customer loyalty. The Cleanliness issue came from Ray Kroc's days as a traveling salesman peddling his milk shake machines. Having done my own fair share of selling and traveling I can attest to the fact that there are some pretty nasty places you can stop at from gas station rest rooms to greasy spoon restaurants. Cleanliness became a USP for the McDonalds chain because Kroc realized that a family on the road needed a place to stop where that family could consistently find clean facilities and, oh yeah, a few Happy Meals for the kids.

So what is your USP? Really, what is it that differentiates you from all your competition? For McDonalds it was good quality food at reasonable prices served quickly and pleasantly for people on the go and clean facilities for folks who had to go! Everything else is marketing and public relations from Ronald McDonald to Ronald McDonald House, their charitable foundation.

My Dad owned a public relations firm and he always said that public relations was "doing good and getting credit for it". Your image is a distinct important part of your USP. It is part of your why.

TRIAL AND ERROR

Years before Rene Descartes wrote, "I think, therefore I am," St. Augustine wrote, "I err, therefore I am." Anyone who has ever started a small business knows that at some point they are going to screw up. They are going to try something that just doesn't work or the return on investment isn't worth the effort. And I say congratulations. Now move on.

Anybody who tries something new or unique is taking a risk. Reward comes from risk as does failure. Failing to try brings no reward. Usually the greater the risk the greater the reward, but certainly not always. Trial and error are frankly a way of life for those willing to step out and do something new.

In a previous chapter, I wrote about the Law of Diffusion of Innovation (http://www.smallbusinessdevelopmentservices.com/articles/assets/fl-weekly_2011-11-27.pdf) that covered the fact that it takes time for a new idea to take hold. King Gillette took years to get his safety razor made and accepted. Most small business owners don't have that kind of time to reach a breakeven point in their efforts. Even the best business planning will not always get you where you need to be. At some point you may just have to throw in the towel or adjust your strategy. The essence of trial and error is admitting when you are wrong and changing course.

At least once a week I check in online with www.ted.com to see if anything new was posted that is of interest. There usually is something and each presentation has a suggestion next to it for the next video to watch related to the subject you just watched. Hours later I realize I've just burned through a Sunday afternoon. I just finished watching a video by Kathryn Schulz who bills herself as a "Wrongologist" on the topic "On Being Wrong".

Kathryn makes a great point about how we tend to believe what we believe and defend what we believe even if it isn't true. Like Wile E. Coyote who chases the Road Runner off a cliff and keeps running until he looks down and realizes he is not on solid ground anymore and drops to the bottom of the canyon in a puff of smoke. As long as he kept running he stayed up. As soon as he looked down he was toast. That is pretty much how we behave when we are wrong. We keep running with our belief until we discover we were wrong then we need to change course (I'm thinking an Acme Parachute would help). You will in the course of building a business be wrong at some point in time and the sooner you can correct your error the better off you will be.

Stew Leonard's grocery chain has a 2 rule Policy Statement:

Rule 1 – The Customer is always right

Rule 2 – If the Customer is ever wrong, reread rule 1.

Happy customers are the life blood of any successful business. All of Stew's customers can't always be right, but you can bet they always believe they are right. Stew's has a philosophy of trying new things all the time. Some of the time they don't work out but they encourage employees to try new ideas. It is one of the things that differentiate them from other grocery chains. They make as big a deal out of trial and error as they do trial and success.

Give it a try!

FUMBLING FORWARD

"You are never a complete failure. You can always serve as a bad example." Joe Baker

Joe was Chairman of the Board of an association I ran as President and CEO in Washington, DC. He was always willing to try new ideas and fail and move on to the next thing. Joe once ran for Congress and lost but took it in stride. He was proud of the fact he had gotten over 40% of the vote in a precinct that had not traditionally voted more than 30% for anyone in his party. He often used the above quote to encourage me to "think outside the box" and as a result we tried some things that failed but many things that had never been done before and succeeded.

Any human endeavor is subject to failure. I don't care how great your talent or crystal ball is, things change and you need to adapt and move on and accept failure as a learning experience. The more new things you try the more opportunity you have to fail. On the other hand, failing to try anything new is itself a failing act in a changing world. Status quo is a creativity killer.

Paralysis of analysis is worse than trying something that might fail. Great ideas have literally been "thunk" to death. Sometimes just moving on an idea provides the stumbling blocks that ultimately lead to the stepping stones across the river of failure.

We all have our risk limits. You never want to knowingly bet the ranch on a failed idea. But, there are some learning experiences you can only get from a whopping flop and you won't really know until you try that it will not be a success.

I just finished reading a great book called The Failure Myth by Michael Sisti. He talks about some famous and real life failures and the lessons that can be learned and avoided in future business endeavors.

He notes that Walt Disney was fired as a newspaper editor for "lack of imagination". Which leads me to believe that it is not an accident that the hundreds of creative folks who now work for Walt's company are known as "Disney Imagineers". Mike points out that Henry Ford went broke 5 times before his successful adaptation of Colt's assembly line manufacturing system for making cars. Bill Gates and Paul Allen quit college to develop their famous company, Traf-O-Data. OK, I've never heard of it either. They learned from their failure and Microsoft was born. It seems that behind every success story is a failure story to go along with it.

Sisti quotes Robert Schuller who said "Failure doesn't mean YOU are a failure…it just means you haven't succeeded yet". He also has a quote in the book from Supreme Court Justice, William Strong, "The only time you don't fail is the last time you try anything and it works".

That's just how it is with entrepreneurs. They just keep trying until they get it right. They try things that either work or don't and they adjust and move on. I like to call it fumbling forward. Sometimes you can attribute success to a great plan well executed and sometimes you just get lucky. Nothing wrong with that, if it works it works. If it works OK but you can improve on it, do it. If it fails miserably, then learn from it and move on. There are always more things you can try.

DIFFERENTIATION

"There aren't any cover bands in the Rock and Roll Hall of Fame." (Scott Ginsberg)

I just read a great article by Joe Wollenweber, who is a senior coach with Michael Gerber's E-Myth team. It included the above quote by Scott Ginsberg, and it really struck home with me.

Over the years as both a teacher of entrepreneurs and a SCORE counselor I've worked with hundreds of folks who took their technical skills and decided to strike out on their own in their own businesses. While you may be a plumber, or lawn mower, or hair stylist, the fact is you are one of many and the more replaceable you are the more likely you are to be replaced. Somebody is going to undercut your price and you are going to lose the business. It is that simple, the more competition you have in your endeavors the more likely you are to have to compete on price. You are essentially a commodity.

So how do you make yourself unique so that customers are willing to pay for your service or product at whatever reasonable cost you determine? What will make folks choose you over all the competition? I like Wollenweber's solution; you already know what is different about you or your product or service.

You know because you know what you like. You are somebody's customer and if you think about it you have preferences for where you shop. Do you get your groceries from Publix or Wal-Mart? Why? Do you drink Coke or Sam's Club soda? Why?

So how do you differentiate? You figure out why you prefer one product or service over another and apply it to your own business. When you go shopping ask yourself why you are using a particular service or buying a specific product. Can you get it cheaper? Probably. If you prefer shopping at a particular store, what is it about that store that makes the difference for you?

I've quoted Wayne Dyer in the past about not dying with your music still in you. Just like the cover bands who play other peoples tunes, until you make your own music you will never make it to the Rock and Roll Hall of Fame. Until your business sings with your unique music, you will never be in the Business Hall of Fame.

I get my hair cut by the lovely and talented Mindy Bailey at A Select Salon. Not only does she do a great job, I enjoy chatting with her. She is an amazing entrepreneur. I love swapping business stories with her while she cleans up my act. I've been known to wait way too long to get my hair cut so if you see me looking scraggly it is not Mindy's fault it is mine. She has on occasion when I've stopped in to say hi sat me down and cut my hair whether I could afford it at the time or not. She has always eventually gotten paid so don't go looking for a freebie. The point is she cares about me looking good (well that may be stretching it a bit, even she isn't a miracle worker). She cares about her clients and the music of her soul sings in her business. Can I get a haircut cheaper at any of the many local barber shops? You bet. Will I go elsewhere, no way, Jose.

Anyone who has attended any of our Entrepreneurial Academy classes knows that we are passionate about what we do. We want to help folks achieve their own "American Dream" and we love what we do. And I can tell you that we don't just hand out a certificate to graduates pat them on the tush and say "good luck". If they ask for our help on a particular topic we either help them or find them somebody who can help them. Heck, I'm even working part time (for free) helping one of our graduates in her business. If our students are willing to work, we are willing to help. We don't intend to die with our music still in us and we are doing our part to help others learn to sing their own tunes.

There is also another way to look at differentiation, what don't you like? Have you ever bought something that didn't work or fell apart shortly after purchase? I have. I've also gotten horrible customer service or a bad meal at a restaurant. I recently stayed at a high end hotel and got nickeled and dimed to death. Sure they had wifi to connect to the internet but it cost $9.95 a day to login to their service. Parking was an additional $14 a day. Now help me out here, I have stayed at Pedro's South of the Border for $49 and it included free parking and wifi as well as soap, shampoo, towels, and HBO.

What does that tell me about me that should be included to differentiate my business? Well I like to know up front what I'm buying and what I get for the price. I don't like being blindsided by add-ons. I'm not talking about "up-selling", nothing wrong with a little shameless marketing. If you can sell me something else in addition to what I came in to buy, go for it. Southwest Airlines changed their whole marketing campaign when other airlines started charging for baggage with a bags fly free program. It is what differentiated them from their competition unlike the unbundling and pricing add-ons of their competitors.

So to sum it up, you already know what makes you unique. You know what you like and dislike. If when all is said and done you are no different than your competitors you can only compete on price. Make your business unique. When you are the best, you have no competition.

HIERARCHY OF HUMAN NEEDS

Abraham Maslow outlined a pyramidal process of human growth potential called the Hierarchy of Needs. His evolution of human progress takes us from the bestial physical requirements of sustenance up to the mountaintop of human achievement to self actualization. There atop the pyramid of life we have found our true calling of our existence. Yup, there you are with fireworks blazing and you basking in the glow of human awareness. You have found your reason for being. You have surpassed the gruel of humankind, you are well fed, sheltered, clothed regally, the envy of your peers with a wall of plaques and citations to prove it. Ultimately, you are comforted in the knowledge that you have arrived.

Now I don't want to spoil it for you, but eventually even Mr. Maslow had to admit there may just be another level. Call it the halo over the pyramid if you will. He called it Transpersonal and cited such things as peak experiences. Some religions refer to it as recognition of a higher self. If you are like me and recognize there has got to be more to this existence than existing, then let's journey forward.

Physiological Needs

At the base of Mr. Maslow's pyramid are our physiological needs. You've got to eat to survive. It was drilled into the minds of the early colonists in this country that "if you don't work, you don't eat." So accepting that you have to do something to meet your basic needs once momma bird has kicked you out of the nest, you learn to trade hours for dollars for lunch. Next, we move on up the pyramid to…

Safety/Security Needs

Your first and most important possession is being yourself. Having fed your face, you now look for surroundings conducive to some level of comfort. You need a place to park your carcass for a long winter's nap and awake to find yourself still in possession of all your major body parts and accumulated stuff: a protected home.

That accomplished, we are fat, dumb and happy — not to mention safe, warm and cozy. Onward we travel up the pyramid of life to…

Social Needs/Love

Comfortable in our surroundings, we start to reach out for others. It could well be that our ancestors found greater safety in numbers and banded together in tribes for that reason, not to mention the urge to mate and procreate. We seek out our tribes, clans, gangs, chums, what-have-you, to not be alone. There is an old saying that "alikes attract, but opposites get married" which seemed to work at least on a personal level. But even in our business dealings we tend to congregate with those who have similar interests.

We are fat and happy and safe and sound and surrounded by friends, so let's move up the ladder to...

Ego Needs

Here's where you start collecting the plaques and little engraved gizmos from Tiffany's.

We quickly learn to find pleasure in getting our egos stroked. We get the fancy car or house or whatever "bling" is in fashion. We learn early on to "keep up with the Joneses."

Since Mr. Maslow's work really dealt with motivation, the appearance at this step is mostly about recognition by others. The point here on our pyramidal climb is that we want others to know how great we are.

So now we are fat, cozy, sociable, and the little guy in our brain has his party hat on, a sparkler in his hand with his picture in the paper, and a plaque on the wall. We proceed onward and upward to that peak of the mountaintop...

Self Actualization

You have finally arrived. The lower needs are fulfilled. You can sit on the front porch with an ice cold lemonade watching the garden grow and the grand kids at play (knowing that eventually they will go home). You are fulfilled. All your hard work was not for naught. You are your true self. Mr. Ego has taken off the party hat and quit being so demanding. Those Joneses have met their makers and you have come into your comfort zone. You are the you you were always meant to be.

Congratulations. You've been there, done that, and got a drawer full of the T-shirts. Now what?

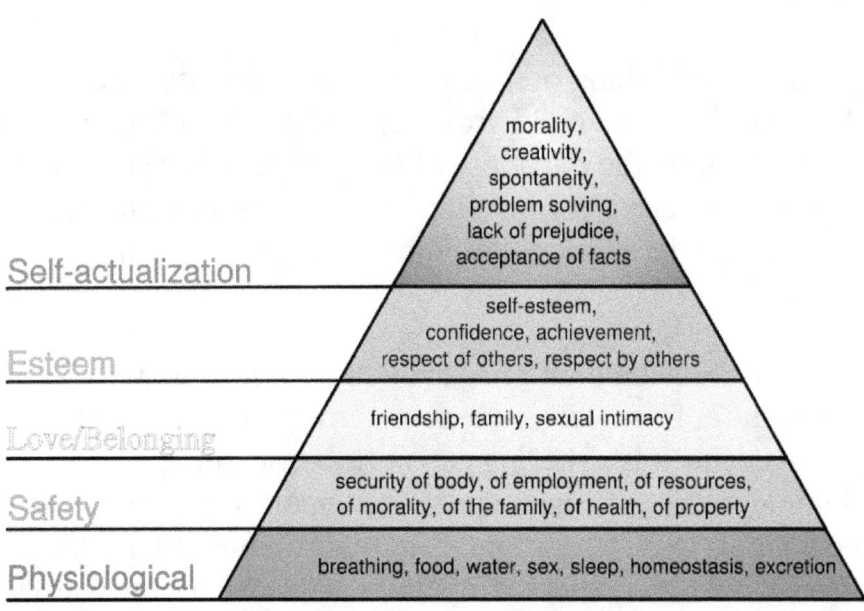

MOVING OUT

At some point, if your home-based business is going to grow, you will need to move out of your garage or spare bedroom and set up shop in a separate business environment. The history of many successful corporations, including such stalwarts as Hewlett-Packard and Microsoft, started out as home based businesses. Facebook and Google got their starts in college dormitories. Apple started in a garage.

A great idea grows where it is planted. But like a potted palm, a great idea backed by continuous effort eventually outgrows the pot.

I equate the birthing of a new business to having a baby. At some point, the child grows up and needs to leave home. Making the move out of the garage is like starting a whole new business with a new level of responsibilities, and you need to think it through before you make the move.

Determine the amount of space you need now and in the near future. Don't let your ego get involved at this stage, because you'll be entering an enormous learning curve. Signing a lease for more space than you actually need can be a killer. Daly's Law comes into play here: "Everything takes longer and costs more." It doesn't matter how many Plan Bs you have — you will need a Plan C: cash.

Most small businesses are bootstrapping, paying as they go. Adding new debt from an office lease or warehouse rental can be a big drain on cash flow. Not only do you still have your home mortgage and all the other bills associated with home ownership, you have essentially bought into a second home. In addition to new insurance requirements, you might have added expenses such as common area maintenance. If you are a sole proprietor, the time spent looking for space and moving and re-establishing your new location will drain your profit making time on the job. It is a real opportunity cost.

One Entrepreneurial Academy graduate, Jamie Lovern of Lola Blue Living, recently moved out of her garage and into warehouse space. Documenting her move with pictures on her Facebook page, there are photos of her and her family stripping floors, painting walls and moving in racks and other furniture to create both office and showroom space.

I stopped in to visit shortly after the move. Her office/showroom was air-conditioned. Her warehouse was a sauna. The candles, soaps, and other natural products she was making could not solidify properly in the heat in the warehouse. Although she needs help as her business is growing, she was reluctant to hire anybody because of the near-unbearably hot working conditions.

She noticed that somebody else in her complex had an air-conditioning system on wheels that could be rolled out in the morning and rolled back in at night through the warehouse garage. Ms. Lovern designed and had built a similar system and installed it. She now has a cool workspace. It was not an inexpensive addition to the budget, but it needed to be done. She and her husband, D.J., succeed because failure is not an option.

The couple had to plan, initiate and adjust to keep moving on as they moved out.

SO NOW WHAT?

OK, you borrowed the money from family and friends and put up your "shingle" and you are now the boss. Let me first say, "God bless you" because you are the future of this country. Now let me also say you have a better than 50% chance of losing all your savings and all the investment of your family and friends, or should I say former friends when you stiff them out of their investment.

Yup it happens every day. Yup, it sucks, but it is reality. Your great idea is likely to fail because I don't care how great a technician you are in the technical skills associated with what you do, if you don't know how to run a successful business you are banking on luck, not skill.

I'll give you the fact that if you are the world's most successful heart surgeon you might be OK in the survival of your business because the word is going to get out. On the other hand if you make the best calzone in the world, unless you are marketing, you are going to die with that knowledge still in you with your failed restaurant.

Look there are folks who make it on luck. Chances are you ain't gonna! Sorry, but that is the reality of life. Being a great masseuse doesn't mean there are folks who are going to be flocking to your door. One of the parts of the marketing session of our Entrepreneurial Academy is me talking about when I started my marketing and management company. When I was selling, orders were coming in, when I was producing, money was coming in, when I was producing I was not selling and new orders were not coming in to provide future sales and future money. It was always a roller coaster of money from production versus sales which produce future income.

Part of your marketing is advertising. If you are not doing it you are not using a sales alternative to your being out there marketing on a one to one basis and you are missing a piece of your marketing arsenal. I know the most effective marketing you can have going for you is word of mouth or personal selling. It works best and as a start up is probably your only option. As you grow you need to find the MOST effective marketing tools you can use that work for your business and give you the most efficient use of your productive time.

All right, I understand that you are now the boss (and boss spelled backward is a Double SOB) but are you using your time effectively and efficiently. Do you need a Yellow Page ad in an era when Yellow Page is getting out of the printed page and into the internet? What is your presence on the internet? You have one, like it or lump it, and if you don't believe me, just Google your own name or your company name. You might be surprised. What are you doing to control how your Google ranking goes to the message you want potential clients to see?

Yes, you need meta-tags and links and all the other things that Google uses to increase your search rankings. Most folks who visit Google don't go beyond the first page so if you are not there they will not find you.

> Unfortunately, sales is often doing heavier lifting than it should because of poor lead generation. A properly generated lead has already made an emotional commitment to buy and simply needs emotional reinforcement and rational support to follow through. This means that good sales is like good dancing: you're getting out of the way as much as you are leading.
>
> —Mark Shapiro, Chief Brand Officer

One of the amazing things that Florida Weekly does for advertisers is to research their industry on the web and pull off meta-tags that fit the advertiser's business. Each of our ads get a web presence and are meta-tagged. That means that if you are a Florida Weekly advertiser you have a web presence even if you don't have a website. The ad itself gets a higher Google ranking in a search because we load it up with hidden words. Some of our ads get a higher ranking than our advertiser's websites because of it.

OK, I'm shamelessly marketing as I also, in addition to writing for this publication, sell advertising, deliver papers, and take photos. I did it for nothing for a long time and they noticed I was making a difference and was part of the team working for the success of the publication. If Florida Weekly had not come along I already had a partner lined up to do our own publication.

Chalk it up to my entrepreneurial spirit as I have started a very successful magazine and have written for both monthly and weekly publications. The whole point is you need to promote what you do. Doesn't matter what it is you do, you can't just open your doors and expect the world to beat a path to your door. It rarely happens. So when you get ready to open your shop or grow your business make sure you look into your advertising budget as part of the process or you might be spending a bunch of time alone in your store playing games on FaceBook.

TAKING CARE OF THE STAFF

A friend who owns a business told me the other day she was ready just to sell the business and go to work for herself. She said the folks who work for her were not showing up as scheduled, and potential new customers were being frustrated and walking out. Not only was she losing business, the lack of service by her staff was hurting her business reputation.

I can't count the number of business owners who have shared similar stories with me over the years. One owner told me he felt like he was running an adult day care center for his employees. I could see where he was coming from.

In truth, it's hard to get owner-quality dedication from a person earning minimum wage.

I've known more than one salesman who makes his quota and then slacks off, even if it costs him additional commissions.

Everyone has a reason to do what he or she does. As a business owner, you have to understand why your employees do what they do — especially when you are paying them.

In 1954, Abraham Maslow published the book, <u>Motivation and Personality</u>, in which he described what he called the "hierarchy of needs." The hierarchy goes from basic physiological needs to a peak of self-actualization in which he states, "What a man can be, he must be."

Mr. Maslow ascribed individual motivation to the level of an individual's stand within the hierarchy.

Douglas McGregor expanded on Maslow's hierarchy with what he called Theory X and Theory Y in his work published in 1960, <u>The Human Side of Enterprise</u>.

Theory X assumed that workers were lazy and unmotivated and needed to be coerced into doing a job. Theory Y, however, assumes that people given the proper working conditions can be self-motivated and take pleasure in a job well done. You can find a diagram of how this works at <u>www.businessballs.com/mcgregorxytheorydiagram.pdf</u>.

Psychologist Frederick Herzberg then took it to the next level with his Motivation Hygiene Theory which said that the lower levels of Maslow's hierarchy were hygiene factors and the upper level were motivators. His point was that work conditions, salary, job security, company policies and relationships with peers did contribute to either "maintenance factors" or dissatisfaction on the job — but motivating factors for employees include recognition, achievement, advancement, growth and the work itself.

So how does all this help you as an employer? Well for starters, as I told my friend, if you go in with an attitude of "firings will continue until morale improves" it's not going to work.

That brings us back to what is your employees' "why." Why are they working for you? Is it just a job until something better comes along? Since all motivation is internal, what drives them? From what do they derive self esteem? What can they be that they really must be?

Here comes the hard part: You have to get personal. You need to share your dreams and ask your employees about theirs. Just like market research for new customers, this is management research for individual motivation. You might be surprised what you learn.

SUCCESS AGAIN

I need to get a life and quit watching videos at TED.com. I've even bookmarked talks by Simon Sinek, Martin Seligman, Gary Vaynerchuck, and Dan Gilbert in my favorites files that I have watched several times.

I just finished reading Sinek's book <u>Start With Why</u> and I recommend it. His "Golden Circle" proceeds from why we do things to how we do them and what we do. His point is that we do it backwards. We start with what instead of why.

The success formula that I have shared in this book of faith times focus times effort (F x F x E = S) fits neatly with Sinek's golden circle. Faith is your why, focus is your how, and effort is your what. There is even a religious connection when you consider spirit (faith), mind (focus), and body (effort).

Psychologist Martin Seligman, in his TED talk on the psychology of happiness, reviews three elements of happiness lifestyles which include love (faith, spirit, why), work (focus, mind, how) and play (effort, body, what).
His hierarchy of happy lifestyles goes from the pleasant life to the good life to the meaningful life.

The pleasant life folks are content seeking to amplify their pleasure and learning techniques to acquire pleasure.

They are happy in the world of play. The good life contingents are successful in their work and content in their play. Those leading a meaningful life know their strengths and use them in service to something larger than themselves. Their why becomes their how and what.

A meaningful life is therefore a successful life as it encompasses success in all areas of endeavor, love, work, and play. Jesus spoke about loving God and your neighbor as yourself. Too many folks miss the point about loving yourself and assume that is a given. It is not. How many "successful" folks do you read about every day who are in rehab? Seligman's first half of his meaningful lifestyle definition deals with knowing your strengths. This might be a good definition of loving yourself or understanding your why. It is hard to love others if you don't love you. When you know your strengths you can see the strengths of others. Using your strengths in service to something larger than you naturally entails loving your neighbors.

Aristotle had this to say about the relationships we develop with others in Book 8 of his work called <u>Nicomachean Ethics</u>:

"There are therefore three kinds of friendship, equal in number to the things that are lovable; for with respect to each there is a mutual and recognized love, and those who love each other wish well to each other in that respect in which they love one another. Now those who love each other for their utility do not love each other for themselves but in virtue of some good which they get from each other. So too with those who love for the sake of pleasure; it is not for their character that men love ready-witted people, but because they find them pleasant. Therefore those who love for the sake of utility love for the sake of what is good for themselves, and those who love for the sake of pleasure do so for the sake of what is pleasant to themselves, and not in so far as the other is the person loved but in so far as he is useful or pleasant."

The essence of living a meaningful life then is loving yourself and others. It starts with understanding your "why."

What it really boils down to is that the confluence of spirit, mind and body in terms of faith, psychology and philosophy make for a successful, meaningful and ultimately happy life.

Dr. Seligman has a series of questionnaires on his website you can access by registering at www.authentichappiness.sas.upenn.edu/Default.aspx to determine your level of happiness.

But heck, if you are living a meaningful life, you already know you are happy.

WAR

I happened across a website by a management consultant named Steve Blank (www.steveblank.com) and there is a section on start-up companies and business plans. According to Mr. Blank, "No business plan survives the first customer contact."

You can have a great business plan with excellent market research and even a great product or service backed by angel investors and if you don't adapt, you don't survive. It is very similar to what military leaders have to say about war: as soon as the shooting starts, the battle plans change. Command and control in business are the same as in war. Ultimately, the customer (or the situation) controls the outcome.

In battling a dictator with a centralized command and control system, the first objective is to destroy his ability to command. There's a great book by Robin Moore called The Hunt for Bin Laden that covers the Green Berets who were first boots on the ground in Afghanistan fighting with the Northern Alliance and directing laser guided bombs to their targets. The first tent they would target was the one with the antenna as this was the seat of the opposing army's command and control.

Start-up business owners have a tendency to centralize their own command and control in an attempt to stick with their business plans. But as Mr. Blank points out, that all goes out the window when the first customer walks in the door. In what will probably be considered heresy by my SCORE brothers and sisters, a business plan is only an intended snapshot of a business idea, particularly for a first time start-up company. I guarantee if you have never started a business, you have got a lot of learning coming your way.

According to Mr. Blank, "A startup is a temporary organization used to search for a scalable business model." In other words, things are going to change and you need the flexibility to adapt to change. I'm not talking about throwing the baby out with the bath water change, but sensible change that meets customer needs.

Salespeople are your business recon team. They meet with potential customers and can give an enormous amount of feedback about what is working and not working. If you are a sole proprietor, you are the sales force and you would be better off out testing your ideas before committing them all to paper.

Now I know this will come as a shock to some folks, but even in your testing of your idea, if you hear great things about it and move forward, everyone who said those great things ain't necessarily going to actually put up the cash to buy. In fact, some of the people who praised your efforts might not even return your phone calls. It is the actual buyers who will determine the ultimate direction of the company. No buyers, no company: It's as simple as that. If there are no buyers, then it is time to go back to the drawing board. It could very well be that you are offering a great product or service, but you might just have priced yourself out of your market. There may, in fact, be several things in your plan that need tweaking.

If you believe in your business idea, don't give up, adjust and keep on fighting. At a recent Punta Gorda Entrepreneurial Academy orientation meeting, I mentioned that my siblings and I were required to memorize a poem as kids. I still remember it:

If you think you are beaten, you are.
If you think you dare not, you don't.
If you try to win but think you can't,
It's almost certain you won't.

Life's battles don't always go
To the stronger or faster man.
Sooner or later the one who wins
Is the one who thinks he can.

Keep dreaming and keep fighting!

THE LAWS OF SUCCESS (PART 1)

More than 40 years ago, I was first introduced to Napoleon Hill's classic book, <u>Think and Grow Rich</u>. I've reread it several times since then and the information is timeless.

Mr. Hill was tasked by Andrew Carnegie around the turn of the 20th century to meet with the 100 most successful industrialists of the time and report on their secrets of success. It took him over 20 years to complete his work and write the original manuscript called "The Laws of Success."

Those laws can essentially be boiled down to a four-step process:

> ➤ Decide what you want.
> ➤ Determine what you are willing to give up to get it.
> ➤ Associate with people who can help you get what you want.
> ➤ Plan your work and work your plan.

Sounds pretty simple and yet most folks never take the time to focus on the first step Mr. Hill referred to as "defining your major goal in life." Sure, everybody wants to make millions and retire to their castle on their own private island, but they are not willing to actually plan what service or products they will provide and take the necessary steps to produce what they claim they really want.

Mr. Hill's eight-point formula is examined here:

Conceivable

Like trying to build a building without blueprints, you will never realize your goal if you can't visualize it. And it is nearly impossible to gain support of others if you cannot share your vision specifically, descriptively and clearly.

Believable

Fifty years ago, it would have been hard to imagine, let alone believe, that iPhones and Droids would exist and do what they can do. If you believe in and value your goal, you can reach it. There will always be naysayers telling you why it won't work. Ignore them.

Achievable

There is an old saying that a journey of a thousand miles begins with the first step. You know what abilities and experience you bring to your goal. Even if you don't have the needed resources, you only need those required to make the first step.

Controllable

Your goal may require the permission of others who may not grant it. So instead of outcome-based focus, you may have to state your goal in terms of your activities. For example, you may want to take a date to the movies and your intended may not want to go. So your goal becomes to invite your date to the movies.

Or you may be in sales and know that on average, for every 10 calls you make, you get one new sale. So your goal would be to make 20 sales calls and achieve two sales. And you may be surprised to find that with this new goal-oriented philosophy your sales-to-call ratio goes up.

Measurable

You may not be able to control the actual outcomes of your efforts, but you can measure the effort itself. Your goal might be to make 20 complete sales presentations a day or to call five potential movie dates.

Desirable

There are many things in life we feel we just have to do. A goal should be motivational and be something we really want to do, even if it is a stretch.

Stated with no alternatives

The time to consider alternatives is before you get started. Once you have decided your course, all alternatives should be eliminated. Rip out the rearview mirror and drive straight ahead with a positive mental attitude.

Growth facilitating

Your goal needs to be beneficial to yourself and others. Zig Ziglar always says, "You can have anything you want if you help other people get what they want."

So, decide what you want.

THE LAWS OF SUCCESS (PART 2)

The second step in the laws of success is determining what you are willing to give up to be successful in your own business.

I counsel people to narrow their options. If you can't decide what you want because you want too many things, your focus will be blurred. And if you can't focus on what you want and what you are really good at, you will seriously dilute your success potential. Focus means giving up other options and concentrating on key objectives.

You might have to give up your golf game and hanging out with the gang. You will probably have to collateralize your assets to get your business going. And if being the boss of your own business is too much stress, it could cost you your health.

Owning a business is a 24/7/365 proposition, and when problems happen, they are your problems.

During our Entrepreneurial Academy orientations, we're sometimes accused of trying to talk people out of starting a business. While we have sent a few folks back to the drawing board, we really want to do everything we can to help our graduates succeed. Part of that task is to ensure that they start with their eyes wide open.

So far, in the first half of 2011 , more than 2,400 new businesses have registered in Charlotte and Sarasota counties. This illustrates the fact that the rewards of success in owning your own business are great, no matter what the challenge.

THE LAWS OF SUCCESS (PART 3)

In the last two installations of "Exploring the 'Laws of Success,'" we have talked about goal setting, deciding what you want and determining what you are willing to give up to get it.

The third chapter deals with associating with people who can help you get what you want.

Aristotle Onassis was asked once what he would do if he lost all his money and had to start over. He answered that he would find a restaurant that successful people frequented and get a job waiting tables in the hopes of learning what these folks were discussing.

Napoleon Hill essentially did that in his 20-year quest to develop the laws of success, which he poured into his book, Think and Grow Rich, one of the bestselling books of all time. With a letter of introduction from Andrew Carnegie, he met with the top business leaders of his era.

One of the key findings in Mr. Hill's research was that each of these successful businessmen developed what Mr. Hill called a "Master Mind" group. These were people who shared their ideas with each other and greatly contributed to members of their group's success. (A visit here in Southwest Florida to the Ford and Edison Estates will give you an idea of the power of these associations.

Ford and Edison, along with their friends Harvey
Firestone, John Burroughs and Luther Burbank, changed
the world in their day with their master minds.)

*Thomas A. Edison, John Burroughs and Henry Ford found great
power in their associations. FLORIDA PHOTOGRAPHIC
ARCHIVE*

Mr. Hill defined a master mind as "Coordination of
knowledge and effort, in a spirit of harmony, between two
or more people, for the attainment of a definite purpose."

Where the heck do you find these folks you can associate
with to help you get what you want?

A good place to start is your local library. There are a
couple of great resources where you can research

opportunities to associate with others in your area of interest. Gale's <u>National Directory of Nonprofit Organizations</u> lists more than 60,000 organizations.

A more business-oriented directory is Columbia Books' <u>National Trade and Professional Associations</u>, which lists more than 7,800 national business organizations. And, of course, there is always a good Google search.

There are many local business oriented groups you can join, from chambers of commerce to BNI Groups to Rotary Clubs. From 9 to 10 a.m. every second and fourth Tuesday, John Gulick hosts a free business get-together at the Microtel Hotel in Port Charlotte. Good networking opportunities such as these might be able to help you get what you want.

Another way to meet great folks is to volunteer your time, talent and treasure to any of hundreds of local nonprofit organizations in need of help. Volunteers as a whole have a lot to offer, and you might just find a friend who could return the favor and help you out as well.

And speaking of friends, they can be a great help or a major hindrance. In building a business, you don't need to surround yourself with a gang of naysayers. We all have friends who take great pride in their perceived role as devil's advocate. These folks should be avoided. On the other hand, it might be a good idea to invite a successful business friend to lunch just to exchange ideas. When I was running associations in Washington, D.C., I used to be part of a group called The Diligent Dozen — CEOs who met once a month after work to chat about issues and situations and share ideas. It works.

At the end of his Power of the Master Mind chapter, Mr. Hill discusses the fact that people "take on the nature, habits and power of thought of those whom they associate in a spirit of sympathy and harmony."

My dad always used to say, "Show me your company and I'll tell you who you are," and "Birds of a feather, flock together."

Even the Bible talks about the power of a gathering of two or more in a spiritual understanding. There is a fascinating book called <u>The Field</u>, which discusses the measurable effects of personal energy fields, either positive or negative, on other people.

The key word in this law of success is "associate." The emphasis is on associating with those who can help and, alternatively, avoiding those who hinder.

Keep in mind that not everyone who criticizes your ideas is a hindrance nor is every seemingly positive suggestion a help. Find a friend or two you trust and get their ideas.

The Laws of Success (Part 4)

The last but certainly not the least, of the Laws of Success is to plan your and work your plan. As coaches for entrepreneurs and young businesses we can tell that we come face to face with business after business that does not have a current business plan. Even a three year old business plan is probably out of date in todays economy. And there seem to be far more businesses "operating" without one than with.

As coaches and trainers we want every one of our clients to have a business plan that meets their individual business needs. We know from the onset that mapping out a plan for the future of your business can be a struggle and we make an effort to make building this plan as painless as possible for our clients and students. We use a systemized approach to helping entrepreneurs create their business plans. But we can't stress enough that failing to plan is indeed planning to fail.

It takes work do the research necessary to develop a good marketing plan, which is a major component of a business. (If your customers don't know who you are and what you do, why are you in business?) The essence of marketing is finding a need and filling it which includes researching needs and who needs what you are offering. There are a number of data bases available at the library that can be accessed by anybody with a library card. There are trade and professional organizations that have information available as well as a plethora of information available at your fingertips on the internet. But the fact is, most young businesses and entrepreneurs never take the time to access these resources and do the appropriate research.

One of our favorite resources is people that have done it before us. If you want to know what it takes to be on the field and how it feels, you ask the players. They have the firsthand knowledge and experience that can actually save you time, money, energy and stress. And many of these folks are ready, willing and able to provide assistance, if you'll just ask them.

We get the question all the time, "Well, what happens when things don't go exactly according to our plan?" To carry the above analogy forward, sometimes you have to step back and punt. This doesn't change your goal that you determined with Law of Success #1. You just have to call an audible to adjust to the changing external influences. It's also called contingency planning or more frequently...Plan B. It is almost always better to plan conservatively, particularly when preparing financials and sales estimates. It usually makes investors (and this could even be your mother-in-law) much happier to see you have exceeded your expectations than to have overestimated your results.

Never combine planning and problem solving. They are very different. Planning is forward looking. Problem solving is in the now. Should you attempt to identify potential problems in your planning? Of course. But your plan should focus on what you want to happen and how to make it happen.

Now comes the difficult part. You've spent all this time and energy into creating this great business plan, now WORK IT. Yes, as you move forward with your plan and your vision, unforeseen things will happen, both good and bad. It's called life and things happen in life. But you should have benchmarks in your plan so you can see if you are meeting your expectations or are completely off track. If not, punt. Make some adjustments. Tweak the plan. Don't let the adjustments change your direction. If you find yourself changing direction, refer back to Law of Success #1 and remind yourself why you went through all of this in the first place.

GET IN THE GAME! GET STARTED!

FOLLOW UP

I told our Punta Gorda Entrepreneurial Academy class that of the hundreds of events I have attended at local chambers of commerce and the thousands of people I have met, only two times has anybody bothered to follow up with me.

OK, I may not be a good contact for most folks, but that's not the point. I've passed out — and collected — thousands of business cards, but nobody follows up. Why do you go to networking events when you don't follow up with viable contacts?

One of our students took my message to heart and made

follow-up calls to four people she met at a recent chamber meeting. She has appointments to meet with a couple of them and will develop relations with them that will pay off over time. Consider this: 80 percent of sales are generated following five to 12 sales calls. Only 2 percent happen on a cold call. This is a fact of business.

Trying to sell when you first meet someone so rarely works, and you are wasting time trying to close a deal with folks you don't know and who don't know you. If they do, chances are they already need what you have to offer and know about you and your business because of your advertising and your website.

If they are meeting you for the first time and they have not met you before through advertising or some other means, you are probably dealing with an emergency room physician and you are the patient.

Follow up is critical. If you don't come with a well-known name such as Coca-Cola, you need to get the word out.

Small businesses don't have big budgets, so let's work with what you have: your time to follow up with potential customers. If your contacts don't fit your target market, put the card you got at the networking meeting in a file. But follow up with every one you consider a viable prospect. Call, e-mail or visit them. Do something to connect with a contact who may have already seen your ad or visited your website. It is all about the number of times you make connection, frequency and reach.

I spent a good chunk of my life in the tax-exempt nonprofit world — making a profit. It is the name of the game: If you don't profit, you fail. So I always made sure the organizations I represented succeeded to the extent they could. Regardless of whether you are a for-profit or nonprofit, you need to take in more than you give out. If not, you can't survive. (Sooner or later somebody in Washington, DC needs to figure this out!)

Follow up is the key to making your business survive. Sixty percent of your marketing efforts should be with existing or former clients. I'm not making that up: Jay Levinson of Guerilla Marketing will tell you as much.

I was chatting with a student recently and I told her to call all her former clients (most one-time sales) and ask if they are happy with their purchase of her products and services and if they needed anything else. But most importantly, I recommended she ask if they knew anybody else who could use her services.

Follow-up involves making sure you have done your job to the complete satisfaction of your clients — and to get referrals.

Referrals are the pre-touch you didn't have and the first of your five to 12 touches you need to make 80 percent of your sales.

The bottom line to your bottom line is all in the follow-up.

About the Authors

Mickey Gorman - A sales and marketing pro, Mickey brings more than 40 years of real world experience to the audience. Author of many white papers and sales and marketing programs, including "Savvy Selling". Mickey is a partner and founding member of Small Business Development Services, LLC, which designs, develops and delivers training programs for small businesses and non-profit organizations. Mickey can be contacted at mickeygorman@live.com or 703-447-8944.

Brendon Sommers – Brendon has been selling and training salespeople for more than 30 years. He is a highly regarded speaker and trainer. Brendon brings a fresh clear perspective to creatively growing businesses through networking, strategic alliances and a comprehensive , customized sales training program. Brendon is a partner and founding member of Your Team, LLC, which designs and delivers customized sales training programs and small business consulting. Brendon Sommers can be contacted at 941-544-3981 or brendon.sommers@yourteamfla.com.